Presents

Learn Piano 2

The Method for a New Generation

Written & Method By:
John McCarthy

Adapted By: Jimmy Rutkowski
Supervising Editor: Joe Palombo
Music Transcribing & Engraving: Jimmy Rutkowski
Production Manager: Joe Palombo
Layout, Graphics & Design: Jimmy Rutkowski, Rodney Dabney
Photography: Jimmy Rutkowski
Copy Editor: Cathy McCarthy
Music Consultant & Audio Examples: Sal Grillo

Cover Art Direction & Design:
Jimmy Rutkowski

HL109245
ISBN: 978-1-4768-6761-8
Produced by The Rock House Method®

Table of Contents

Words From the Author 3
Digital eBook 4
The Rock House Learning System 5
Icon Key 5

The Grand Staff 6
Johnny Blues Man 7
A Day at the Beach 7
Purple Phraze 8
Amanda Lynn 8
The Rhythm Pyramid 9
Two for One 10
The Arkansas Traveler 10
Kum-Ba-Ya 12
The New Years Song 13
Ode to Joy 14
Turkey in the Straw 15
Row, Row Your Boat 16
Bridal March 17
Your First Chords 18
Playing Chords Across the Keyboard 19
Your First Chord Progression 20
Sustain & Damper Pedal 21
Single Note Exercises 22
Intervals: Whole & Half Steps 25
Intervals: 2nds 25
2nds Etude 26
Intervals: 3rds 26
3rds Etude 27
Seeing Intervals 28
Alternate Fingerings 28
Brahms' Lullaby 29
This Land is Your Land 30
Intervals: 4ths & 5ths 31
4ths Etude 32
5ths Etude 32
Oh! Susanna 33
America (My Country Tis of Thee) 34
Kum-Ba-Ya 35
The Major Scale Formula 36
Playing the C Major Scale 37
Descending Cross Over 38
C Major Scale Left Hand 38
G Major Chord 40
The I – IV – V Chords 40
Adding Bass Notes 41
The I – IV – V 12 Bar Blues 42
Chord Inversions 43
The Blues Shuffle 44
Canon 45
Dreaming Messiah 46
Primary Chords 47
Sixteenth Notes 48
Single Note Exercises #2 48
The Star Spangled Banner 52
Fermata 53
Spring 54

Appendix 55
Musical Words 56
Word Search 57
Crossword Puzzle 58
Chord Glossary 59
About the Author 67

Words from the Author

To learn a new language you take small steps, progressively increasing your knowledge until you speak it fluidly. Music is the language you are learning. With consistent practice this book will take you to the next level, attaining your goal to play music. In this book you will learn the important basics to build a solid foundation of music. Don't just play; take time to listen to what you are playing as well as other musicians. When your ears hear and understand music, your fingers will respond. So let's get to our pianos, open our ears and mind and play music.

John McCarthy

Digital eBook

When you register this product at the *Lesson Support* site RockHouseSchool.com, you will receive a digital version of this book. This interactive eBook can be used on all devices that support Adobe PDF. This will allow you to access your book using the latest portable technology any time you want.

The Rock House Method Learning System

This learning system can be used on your own or guided by a teacher. Be sure to register for your free lesson support at RockHouseSchool.com. Your member number can be found inside the cover of this book.

***Lesson Support* Site:** Once registered, you can use this fully interactive site along with your product to enhance your learning experience, expand your knowledge, link with instructors, and connect with a community of people around the world who are learning to play music using The Rock House Method®.

Gear Education Video: Walking into a music store can be an intimidating endeavor for someone starting out. To help you, Rock House has a series of videos to educate you on some of the gear you will encounter as you start your musical journey.

Quizzes: Each level of the curriculum contains multiple quizzes to gauge your progress. When you see a quiz icon go to the *Lesson Support* site and take the quiz. It will be graded and emailed to you for review.

Audio Examples & Play Along Tracks: Demonstrations of how each lesson should sound and full band backing tracks to play certain lessons over. These audio tracks are available on the accompanying mp3 CD.

Icon Key

These tell you there is additional information and learning utilities available at RockHouseSchool.com to support that lesson.

Backing Track

Backing track icons are placed on lessons where there is an audio demonstration to let you hear what that lesson should sound like or a backing track to play the lesson over. Use these audio tracks to guide you through the lessons. **This is an mp3 CD, it can be played on any computer and all mp3 disc compatible playback devices.**

Metronome

Metronome icons are placed next to the examples that we recommend you practice using a metronome. You can download a free, adjustable metronome on the *Lesson Support* site.

Worksheet

Worksheets are a great tool to help you thoroughly learn and understand music. These worksheets can be downloaded at the *Lesson Support* site.

The Grand Staff

Piano music is written on a grand staff. This staff combines the treble and bass staffs together. They are connected by bar lines and a brace.

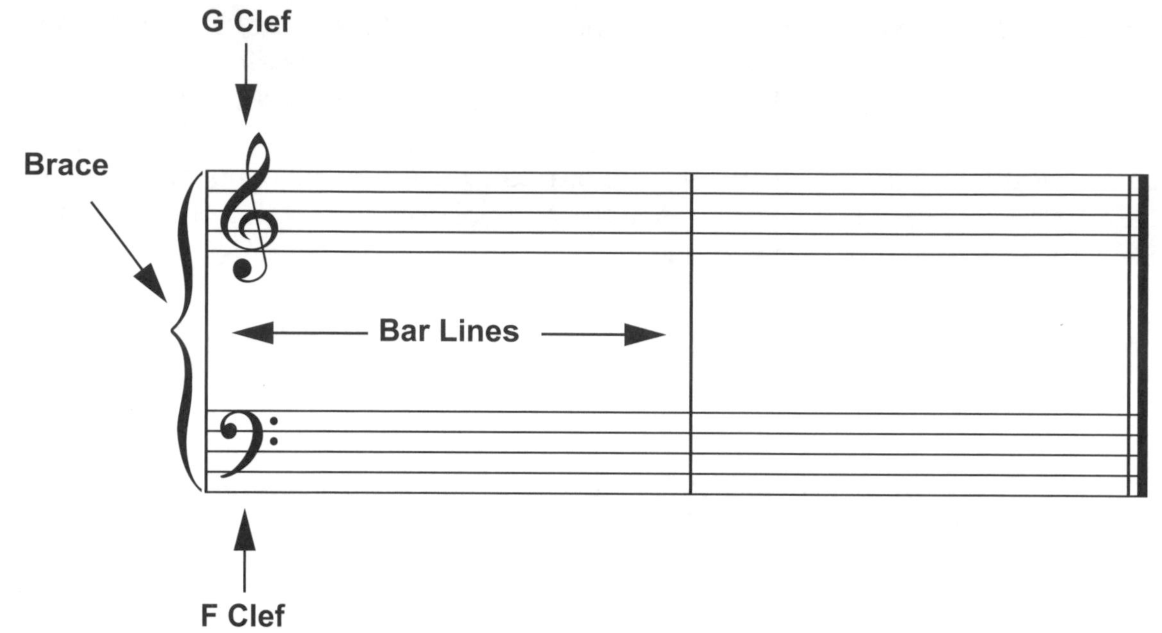

Below are the notes on the grand staff. Use the diagram so you can see where they fall on your piano's keyboard.

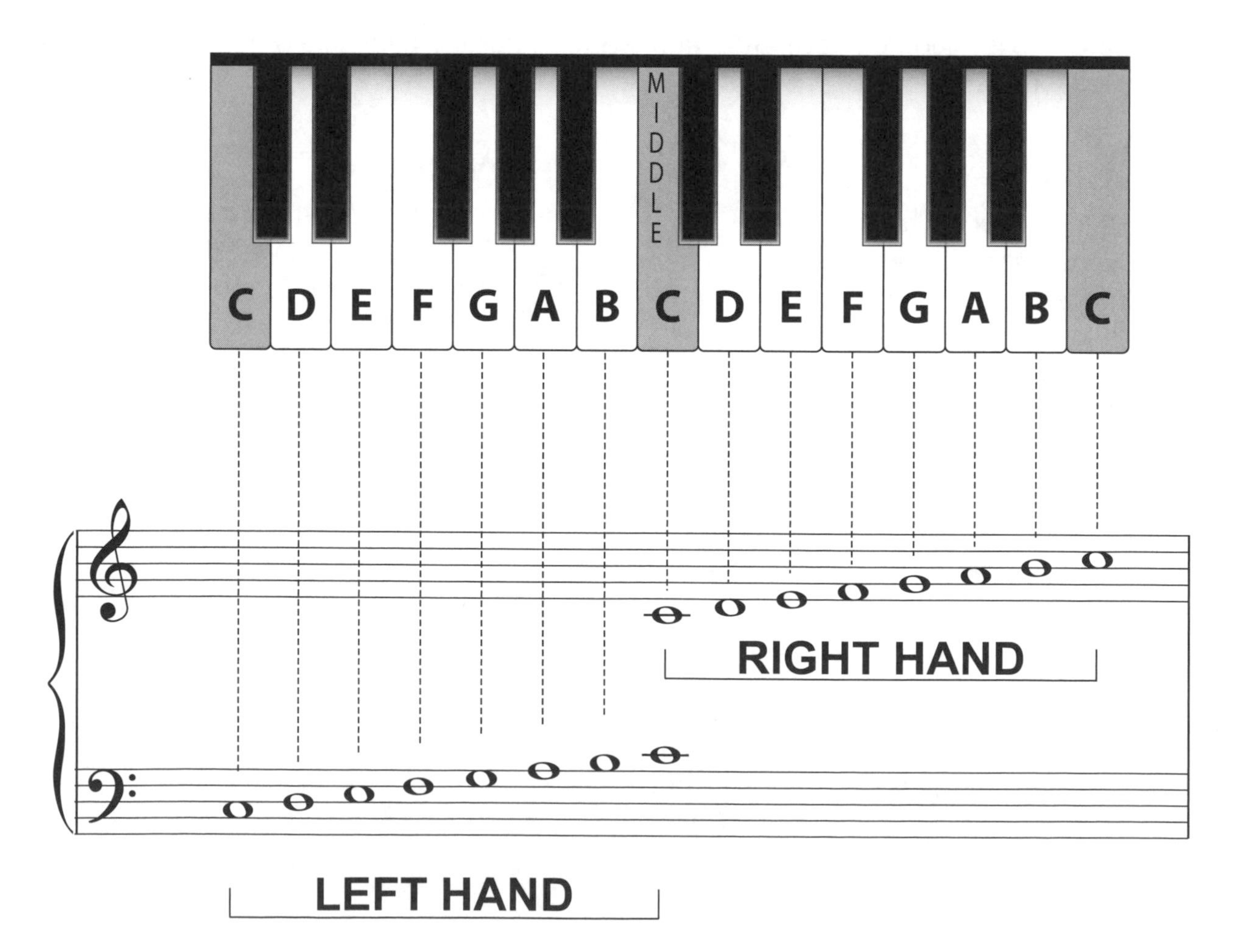

Johnny Blues Man

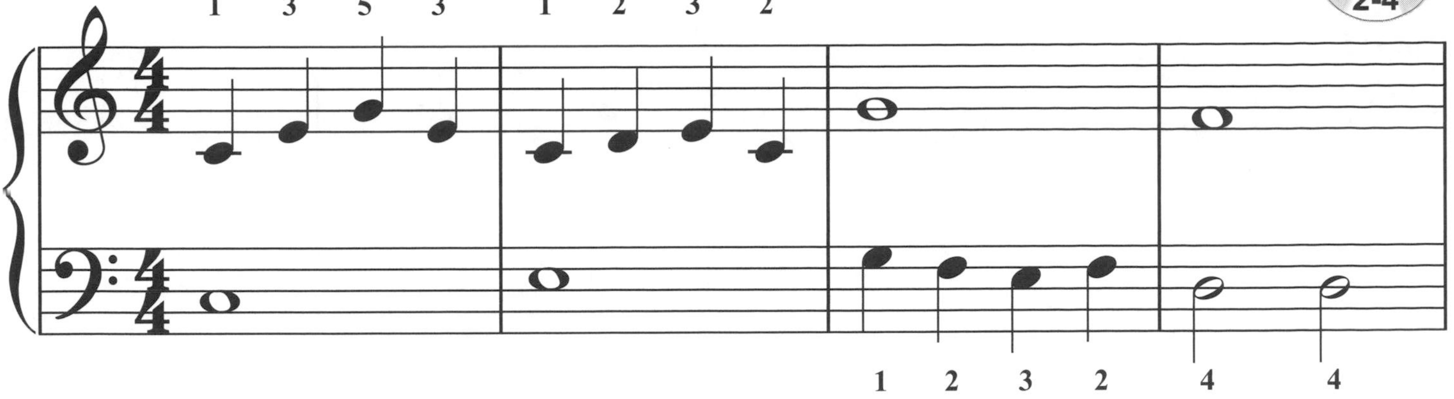

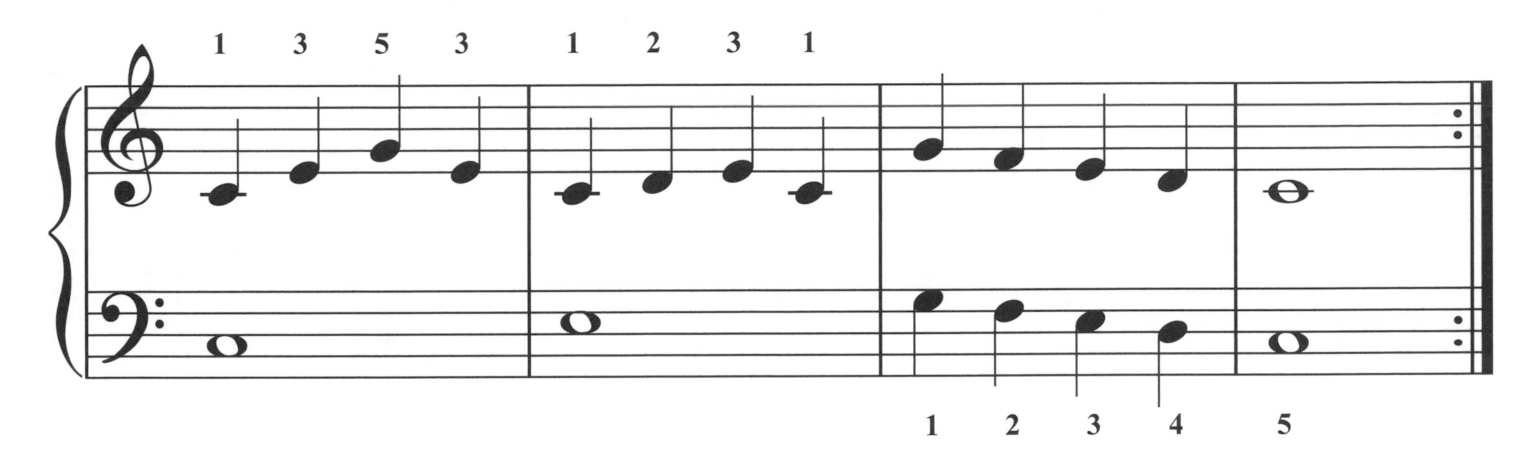

A Day at the Beach

CD Track 5-6

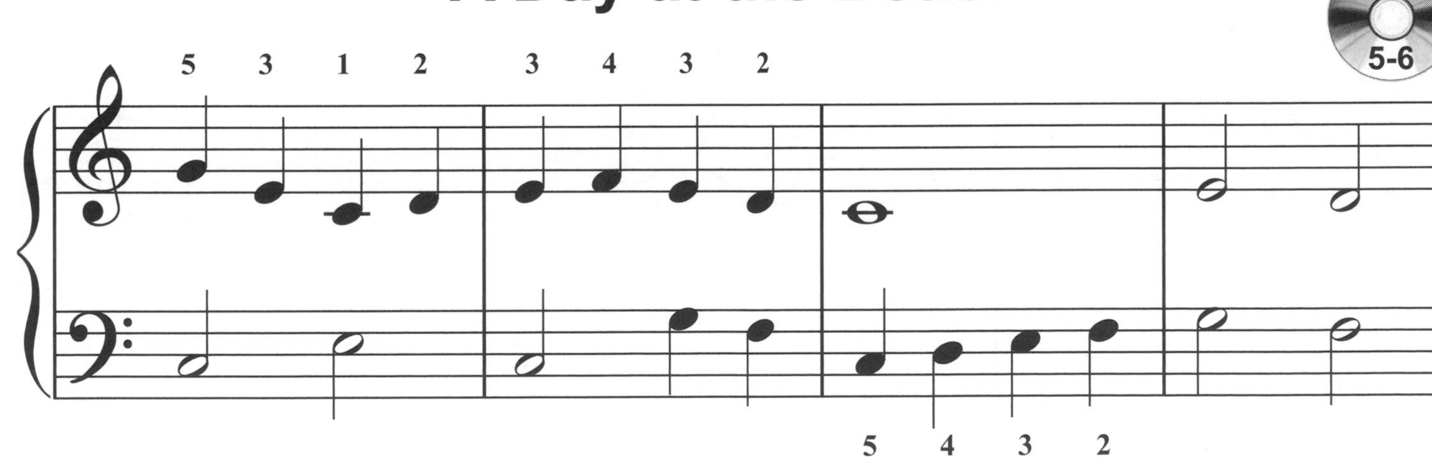

Purple Phraze

CD Track 7

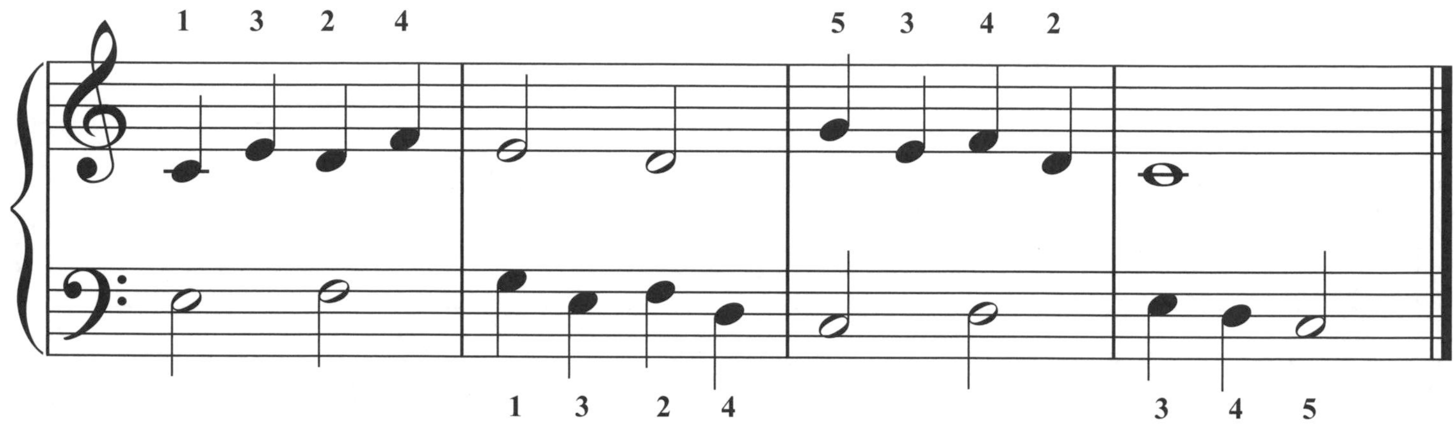

Amanda Lynn

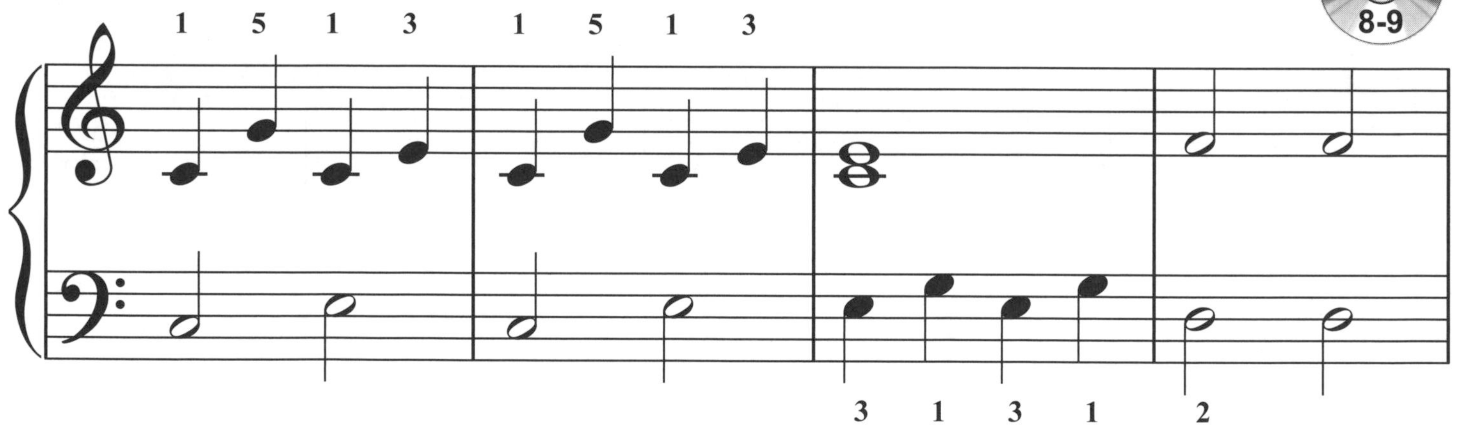

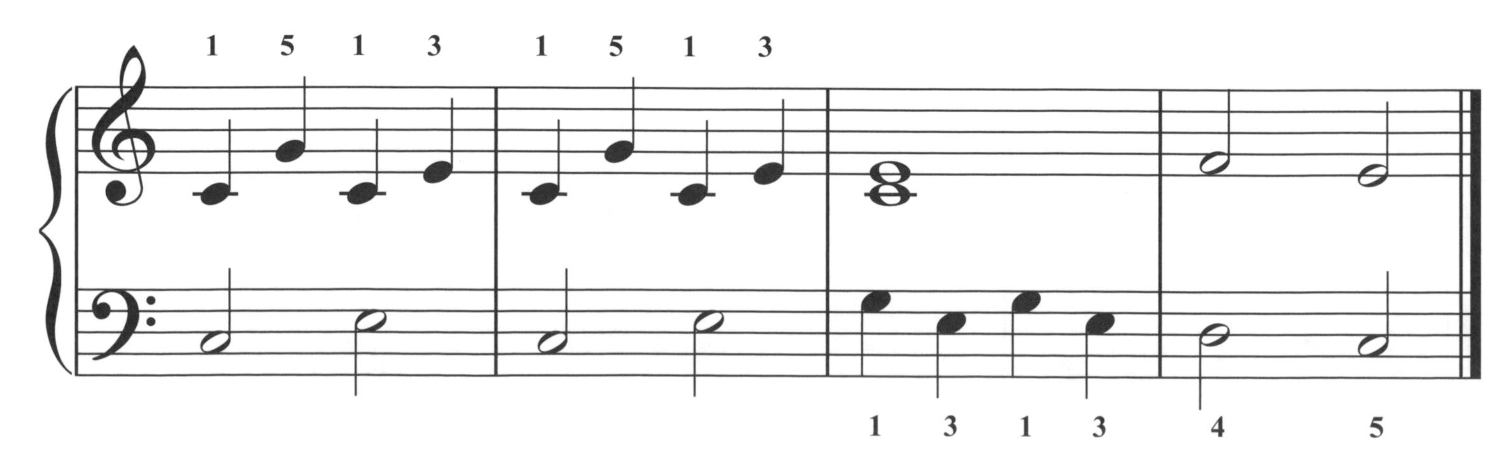

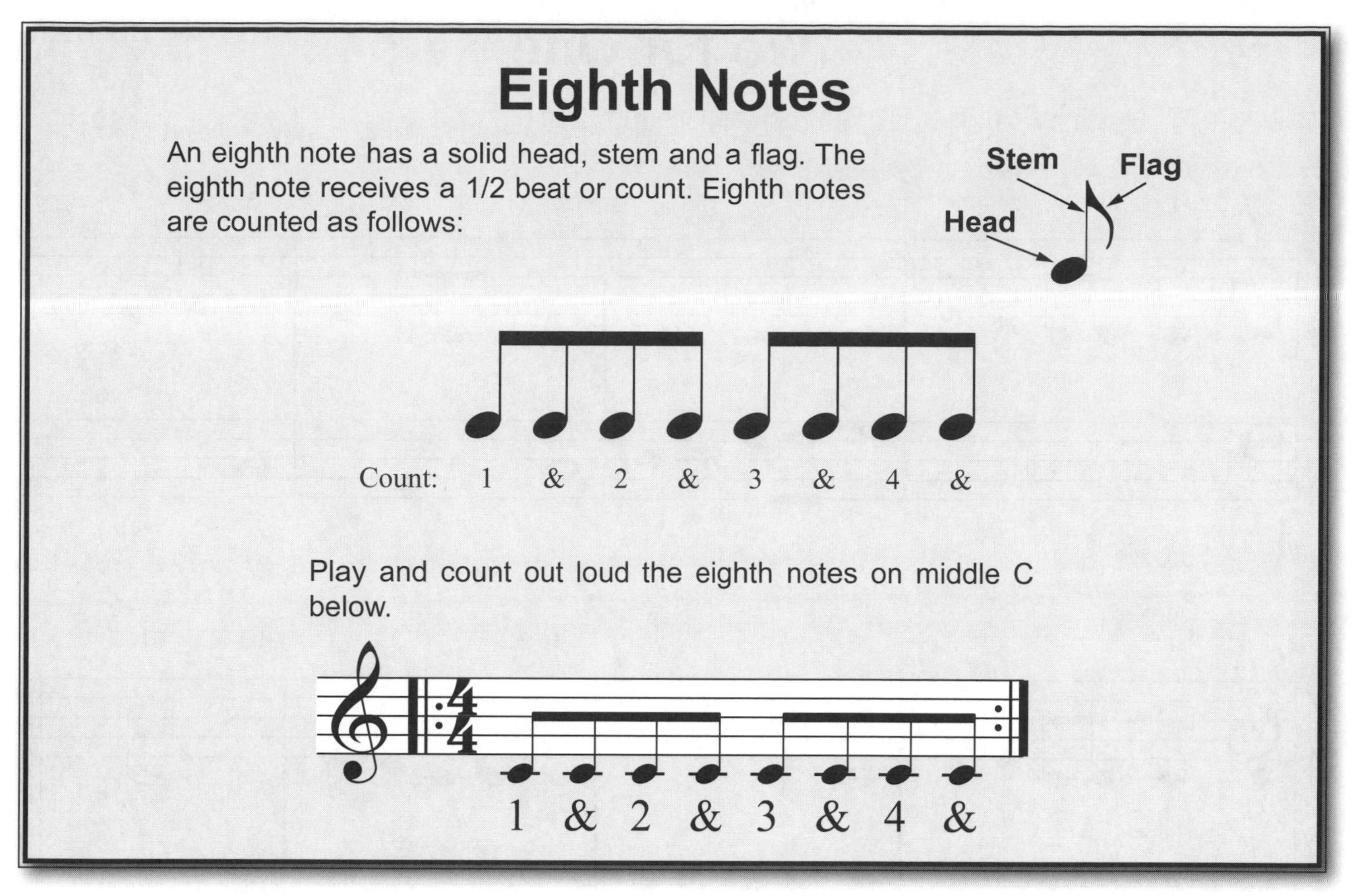

The Rhythm Pyramid

The following diagram breaks down the note values you have learned. This diagram is known as the rhythm pyramid. At the top of the pyramid is the whole note which receives four beats, as you travel towards the bottom of the pyramid the note division keeps dividing in half. For example, the whole note is divided in half and becomes two half notes receiving two beats each, then half note divides into two equal parts of one beat each, 2 quarter notes, etc.

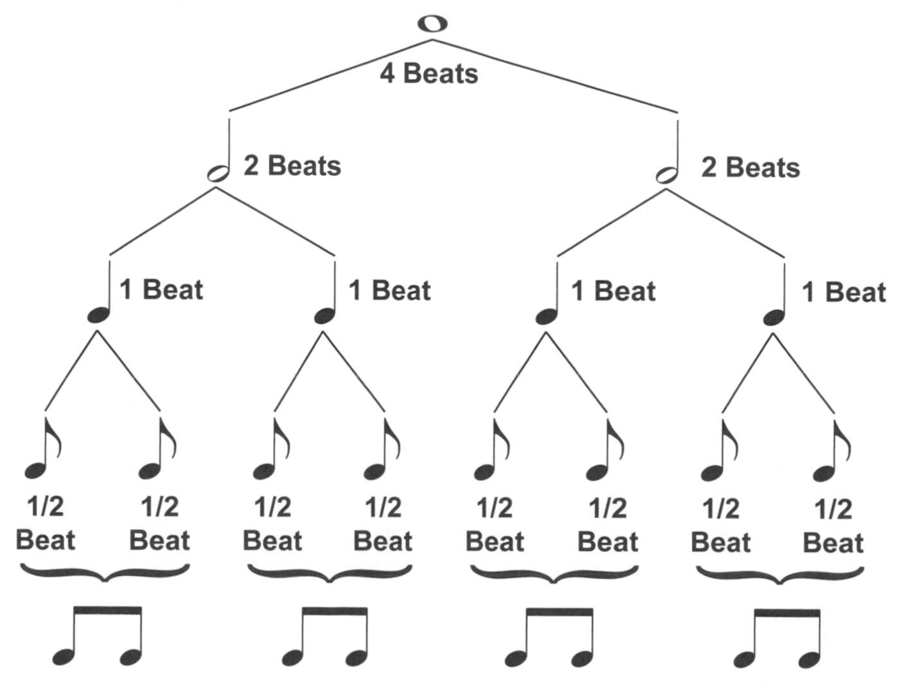

Two for One

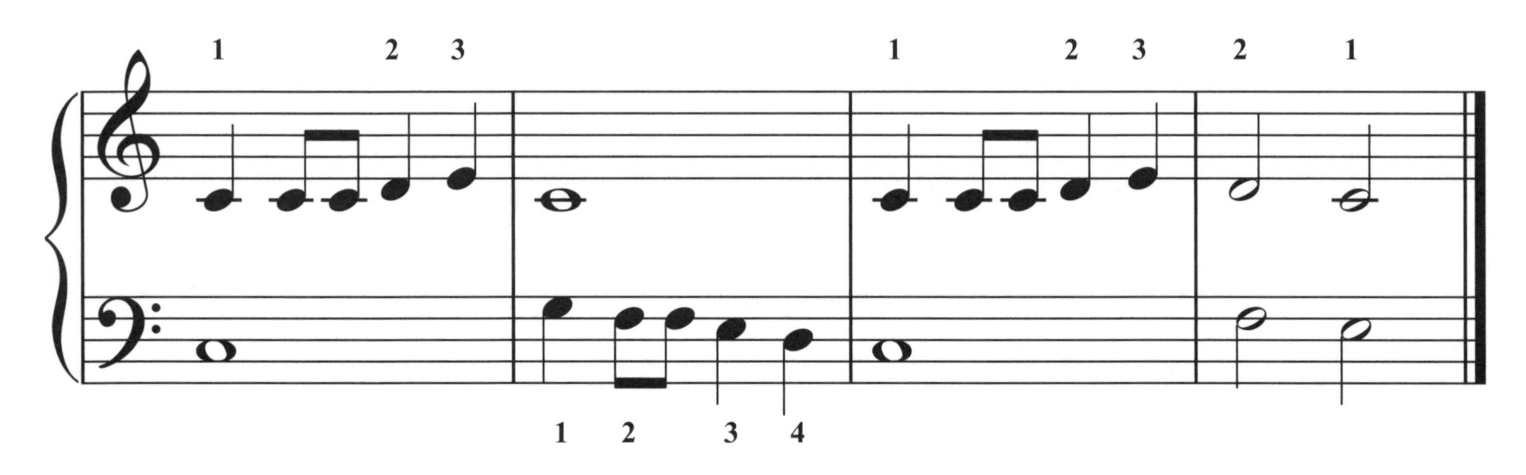

The Arkansas Traveler

CD Track
12-14

Be sure to take notice that this song is played with the “Two Thumbs on C” hand positioning.

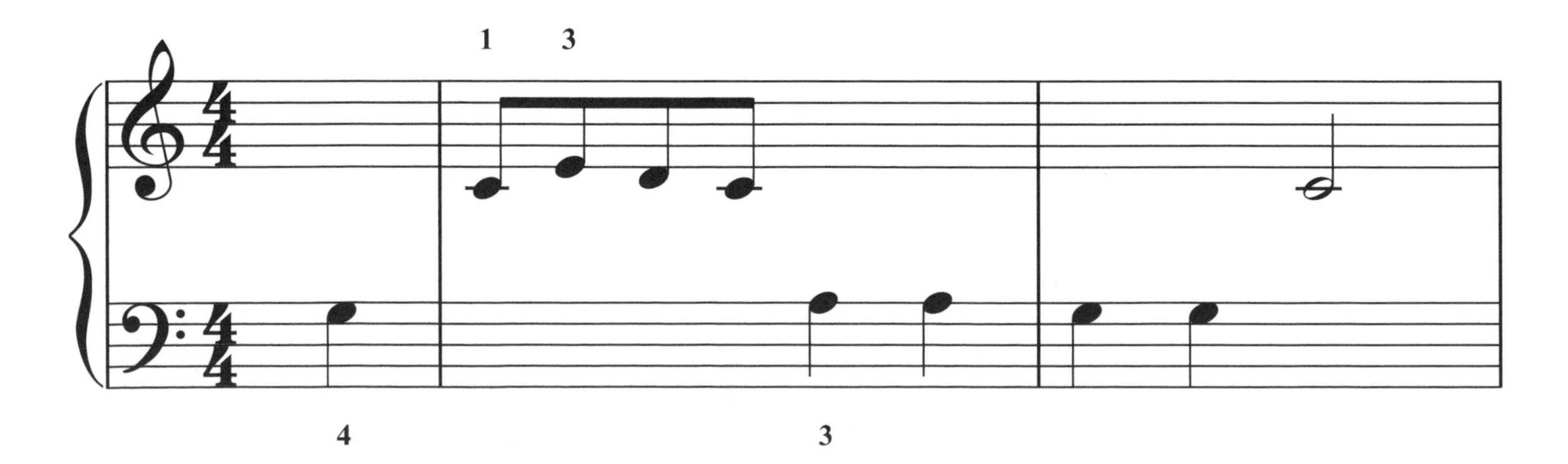

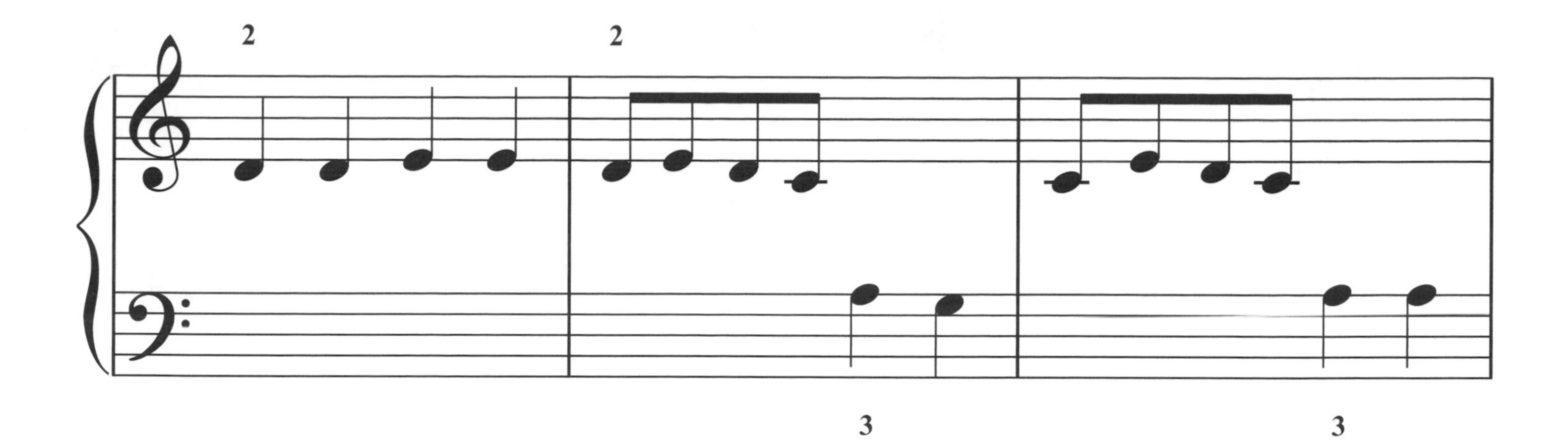

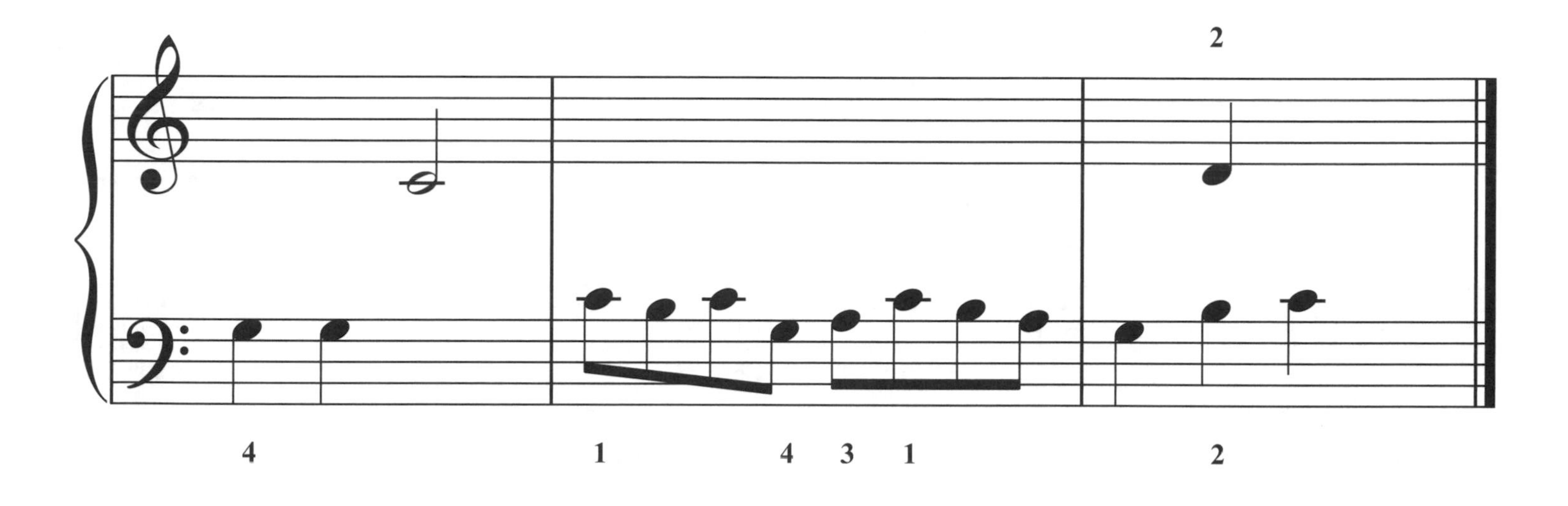

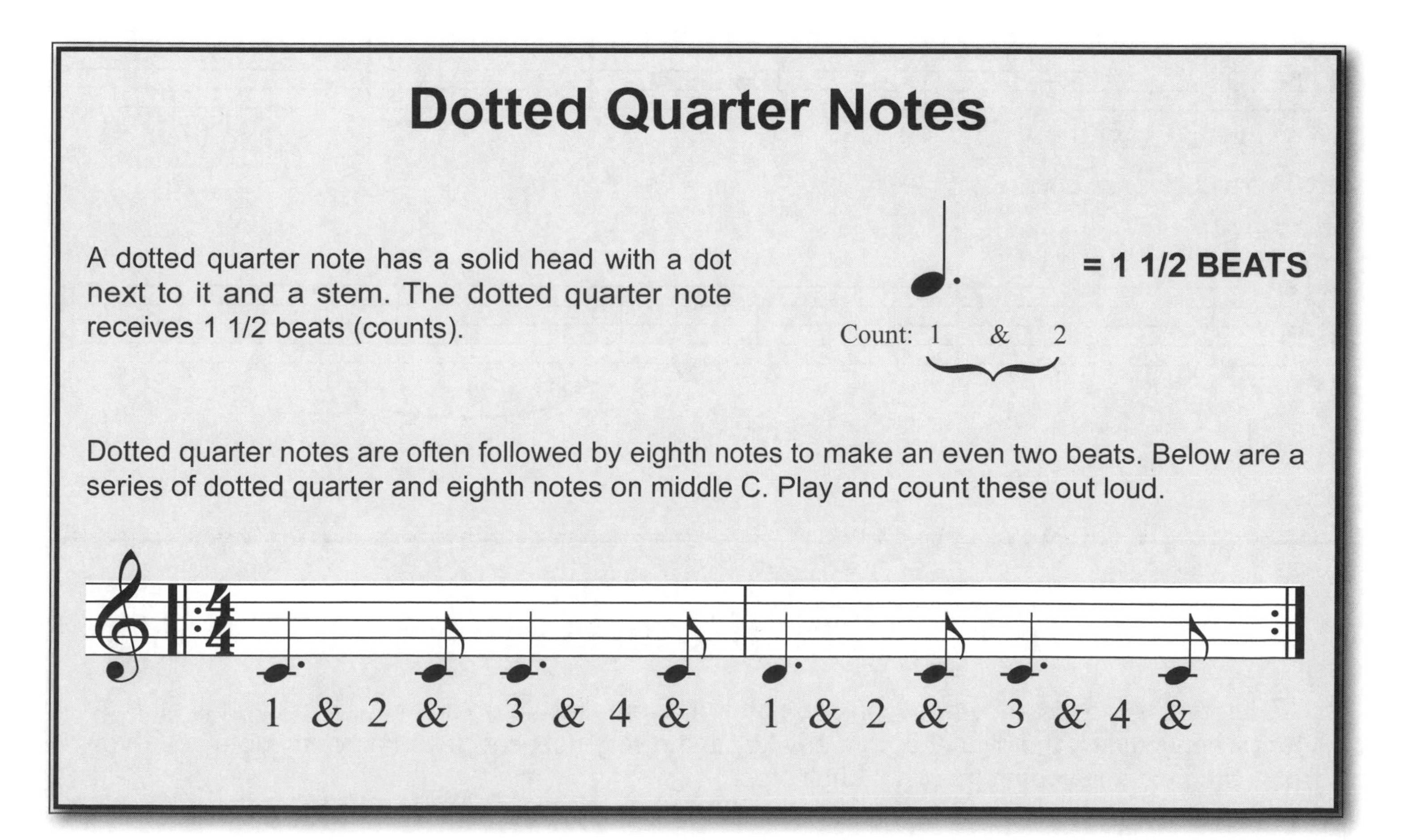

Dotted Quarter Notes

A dotted quarter note has a solid head with a dot next to it and a stem. The dotted quarter note receives 1 1/2 beats (counts).

= 1 1/2 BEATS

Dotted quarter notes are often followed by eighth notes to make an even two beats. Below are a series of dotted quarter and eighth notes on middle C. Play and count these out loud.

Kum-Ba-Ya

CD Track 15-17

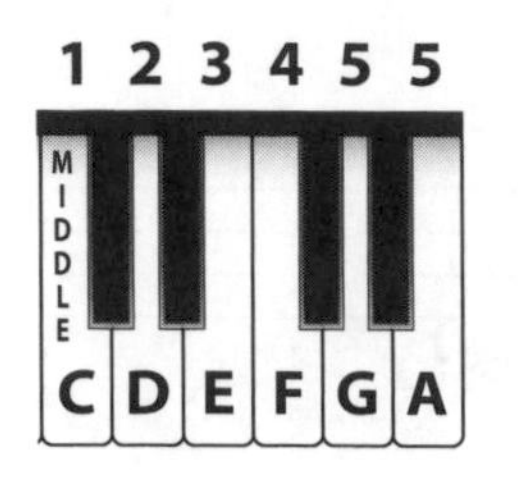

In this song you will extend your right hand notes to play an A note. See where this A note is on the keyboard diagram. You will play both the G and A notes with your right hand 5th finger.

Moderato

African Folk Hymn

Half Steps

W

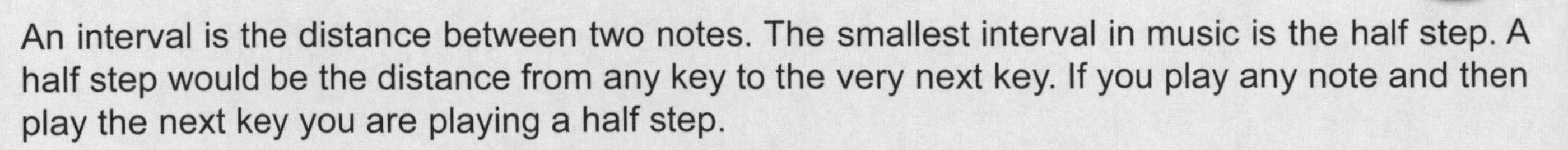
An interval is the distance between two notes. The smallest interval in music is the half step. A half step would be the distance from any key to the very next key. If you play any note and then play the next key you are playing a half step.

The New Years Song

Sometimes when playing a song you will have to use one finger for two keys to expand the range. In this song you will use this technique with both hands. In measure two, finger one will play the C and B notes. In measure five, you play the A note with your right hand fifth finger. In the eighth measure you will play the G and the A notes with your left hand first finger. See where these sections are noted within the song in grey and pay close attention to the fingering.

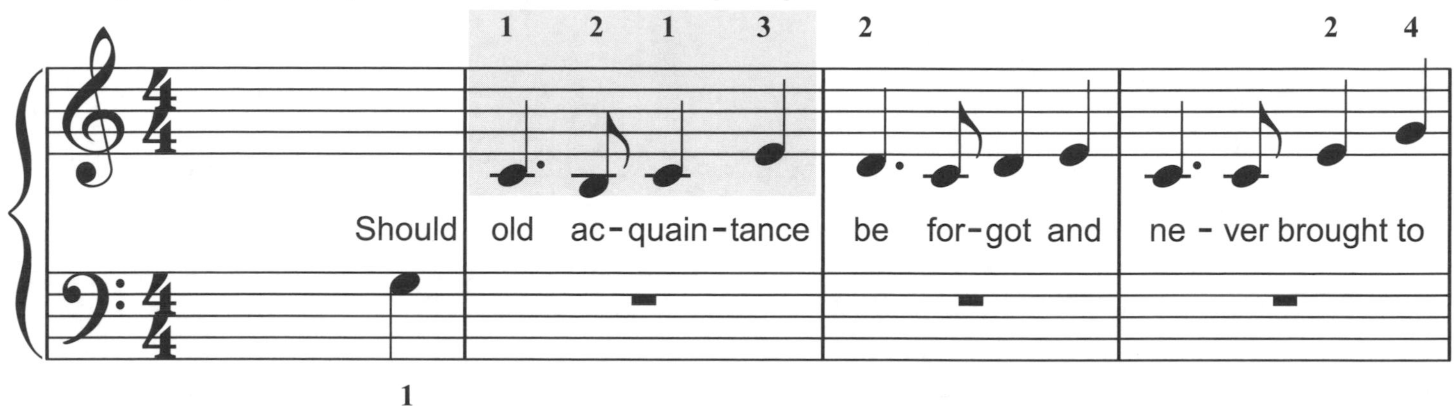

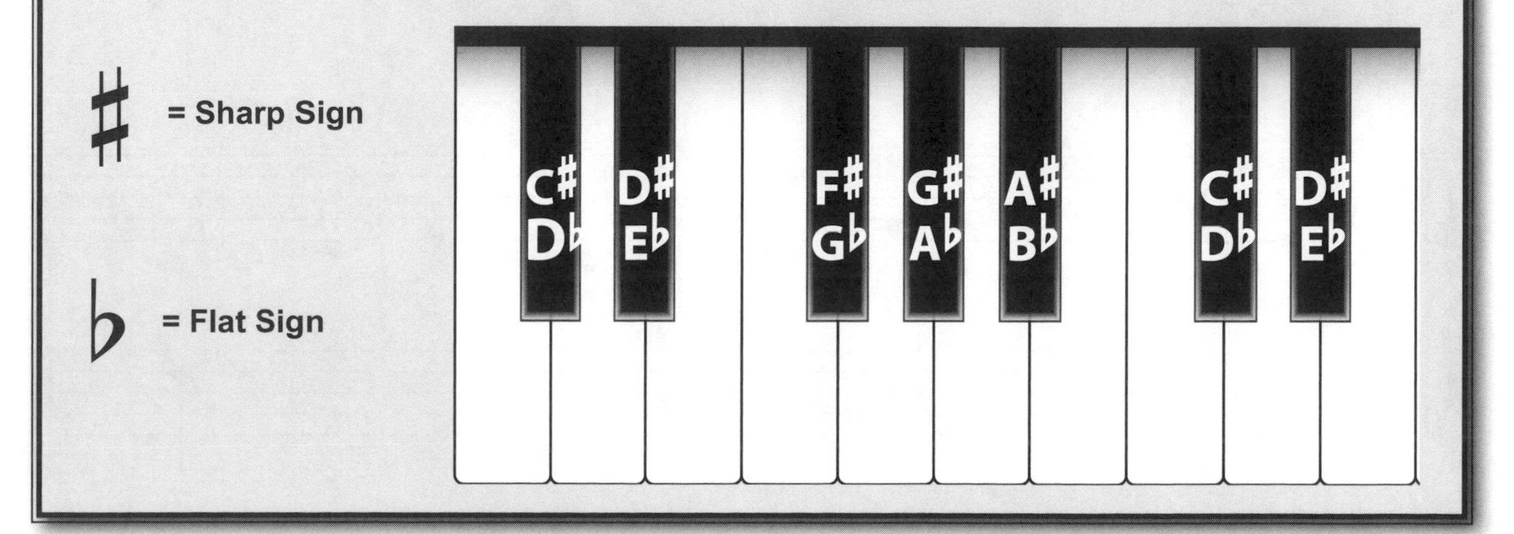

Ode to Joy

Ludwig Van Beethoven

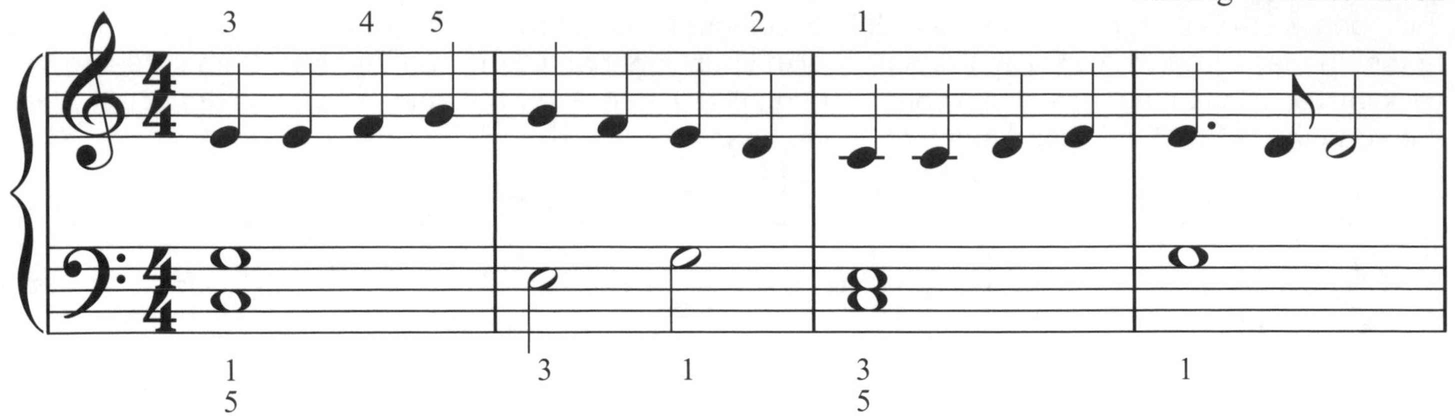

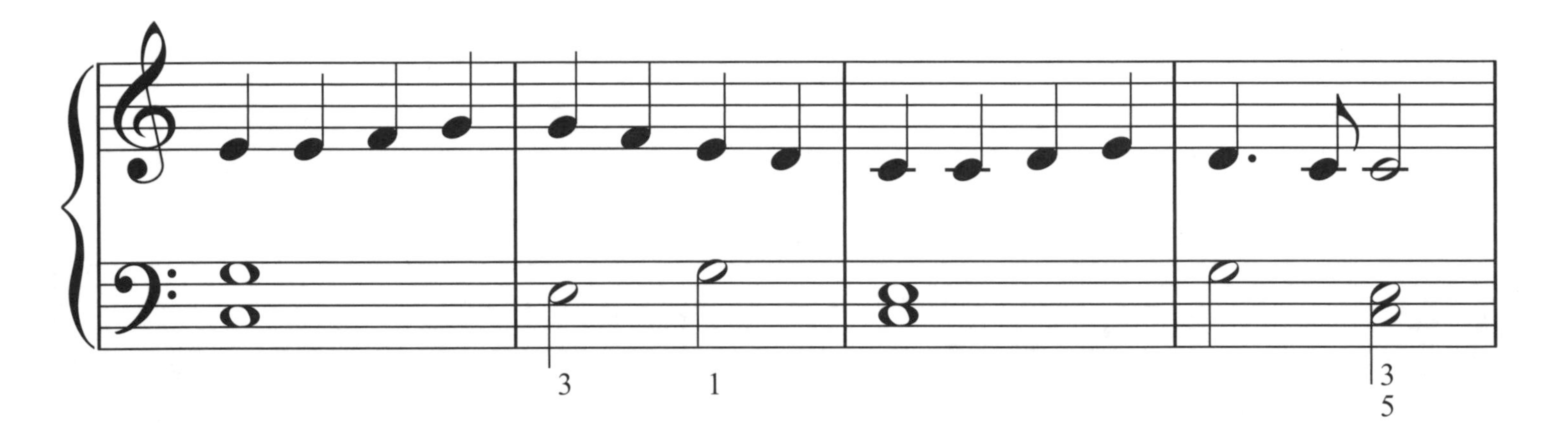

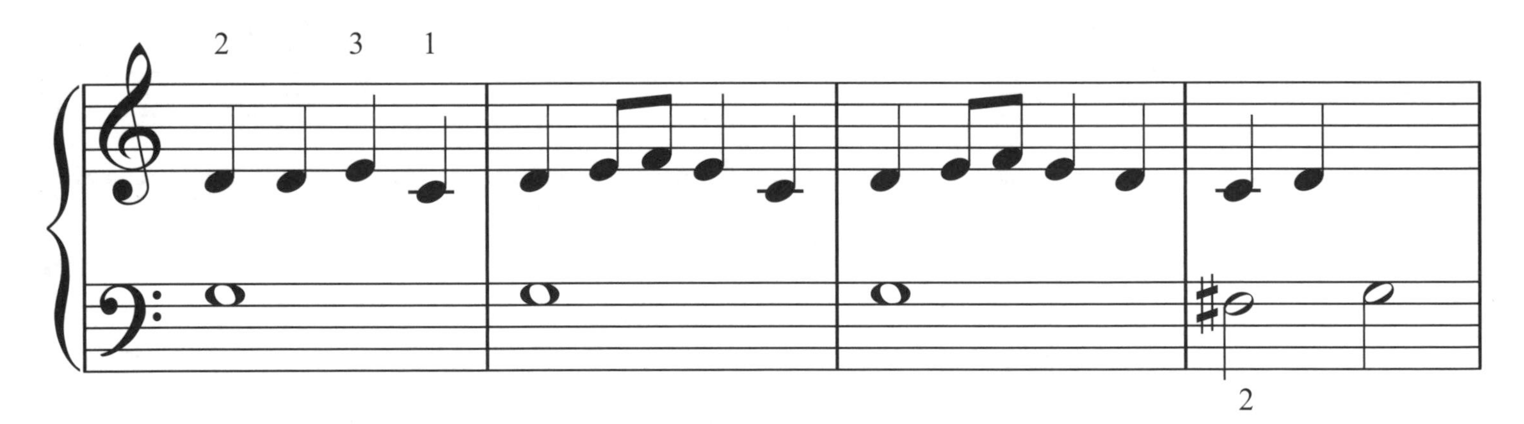

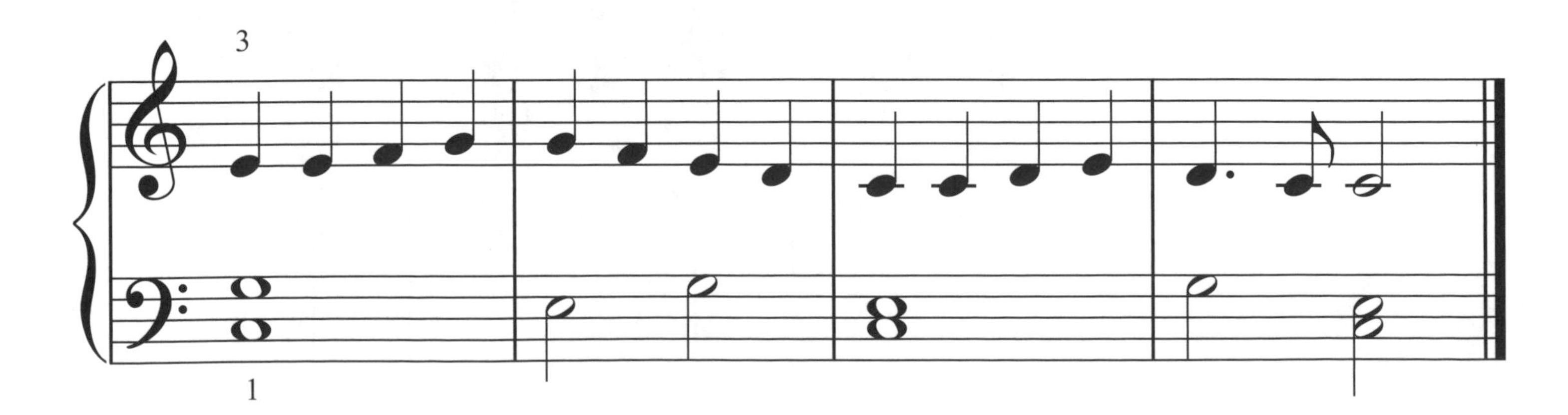

Staccato

Staccato is a small dot placed on top or bottom of a note that indicates that you cut the note short and detached not letting it ring out.

CD Track 24-26

Turkey in the Straw

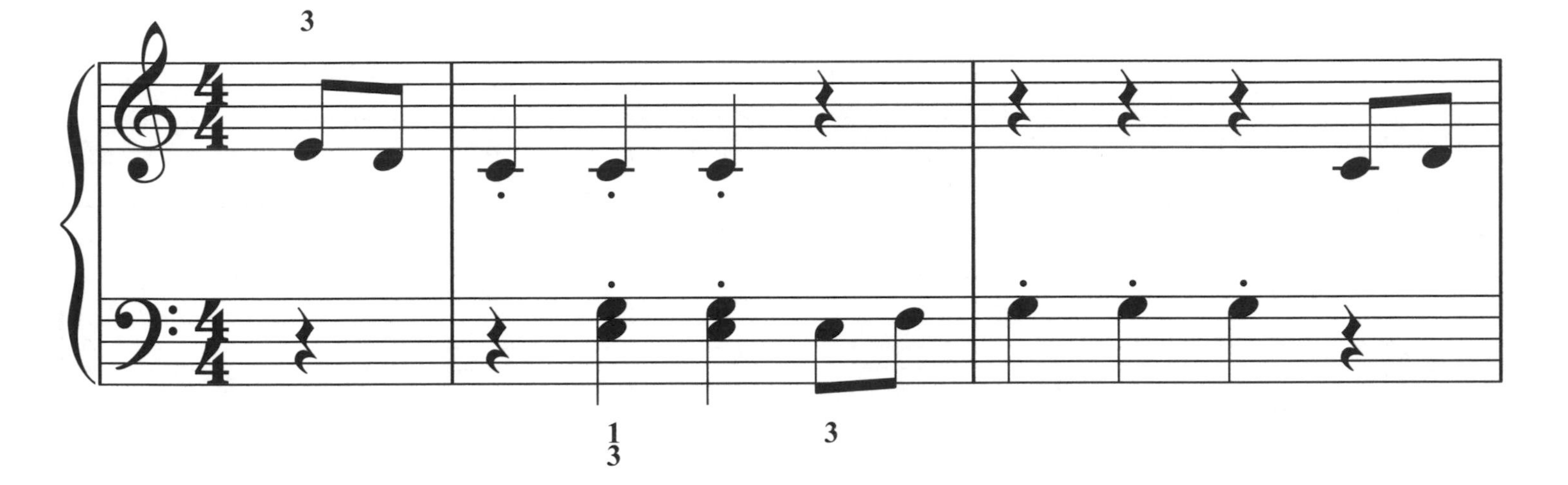

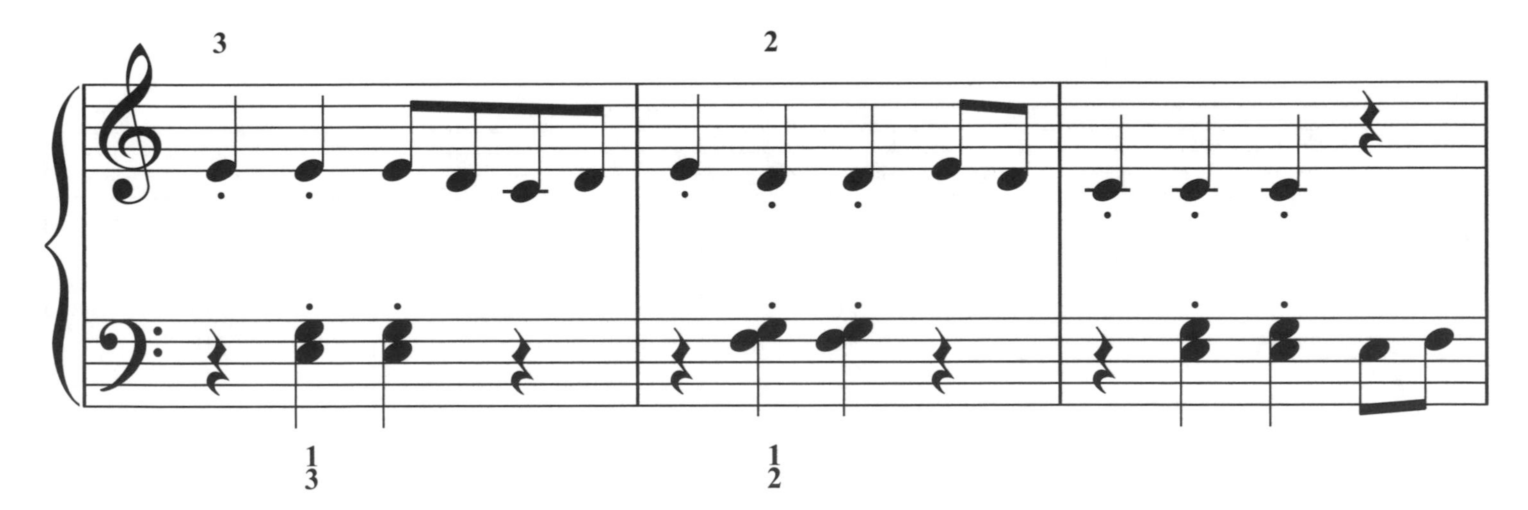

Row, Row, Row Your Boat

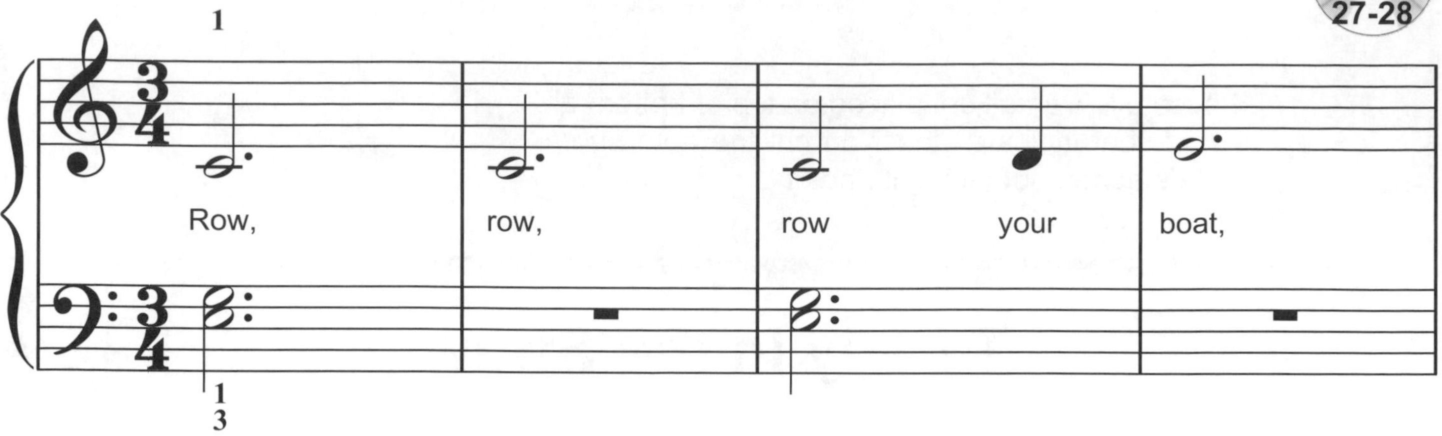

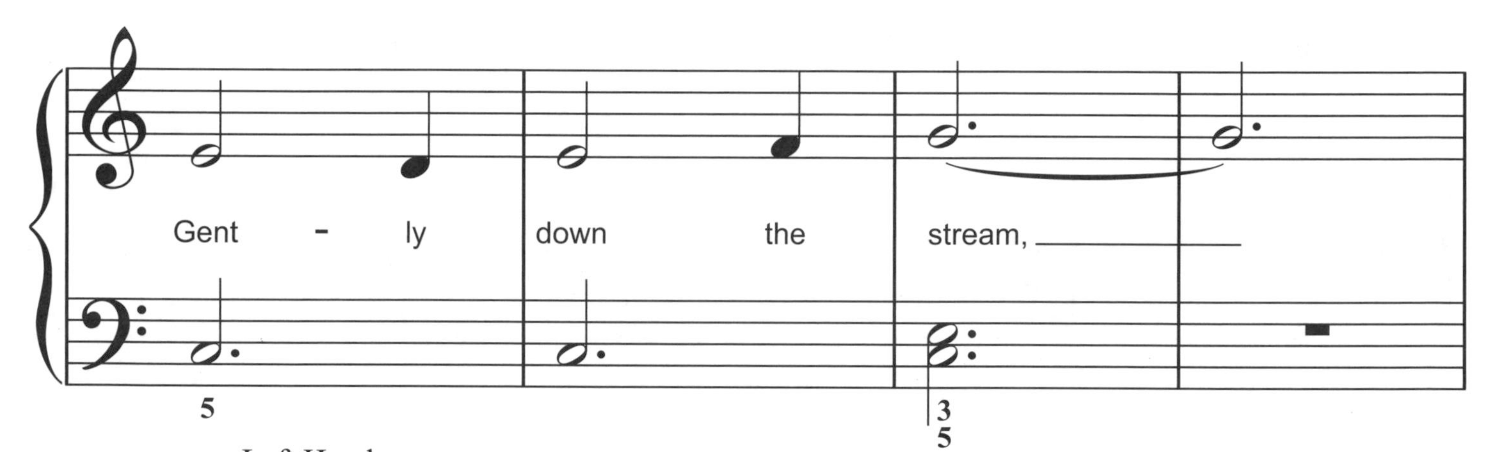

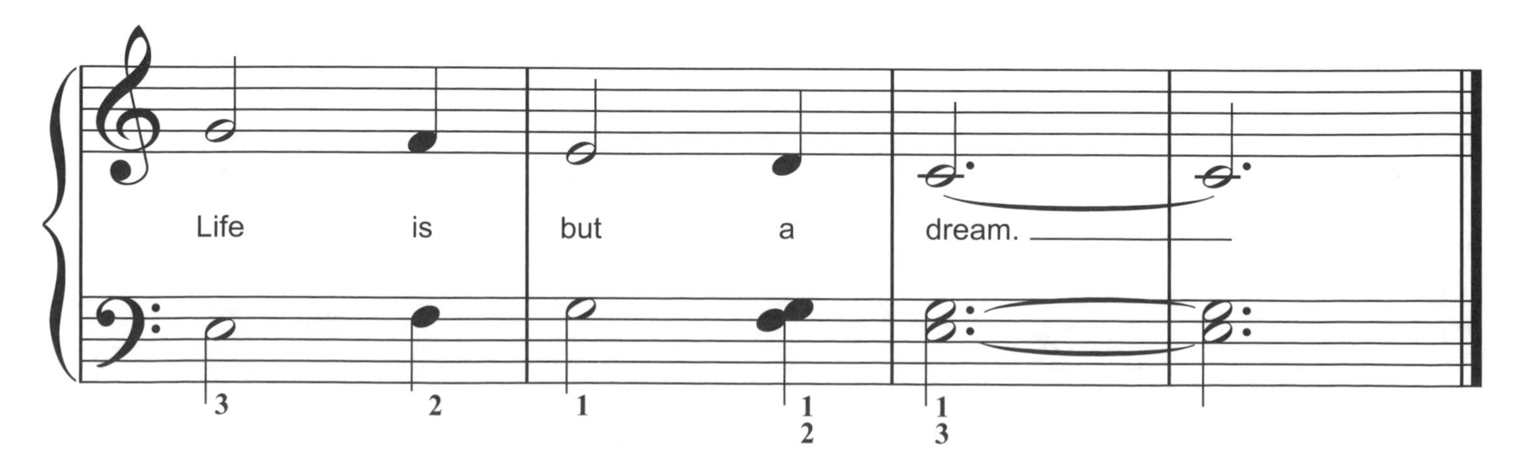

Bridal March

In this song there will be two right hand variations. In measure two you will shift down to play the B and C with your first and second fingers. In measure four there is a right hand cross over. To play the B note cross your second finger over your first finger to play that note then swing it back to play the D note. I have depicted these notes with circles around the finger number.

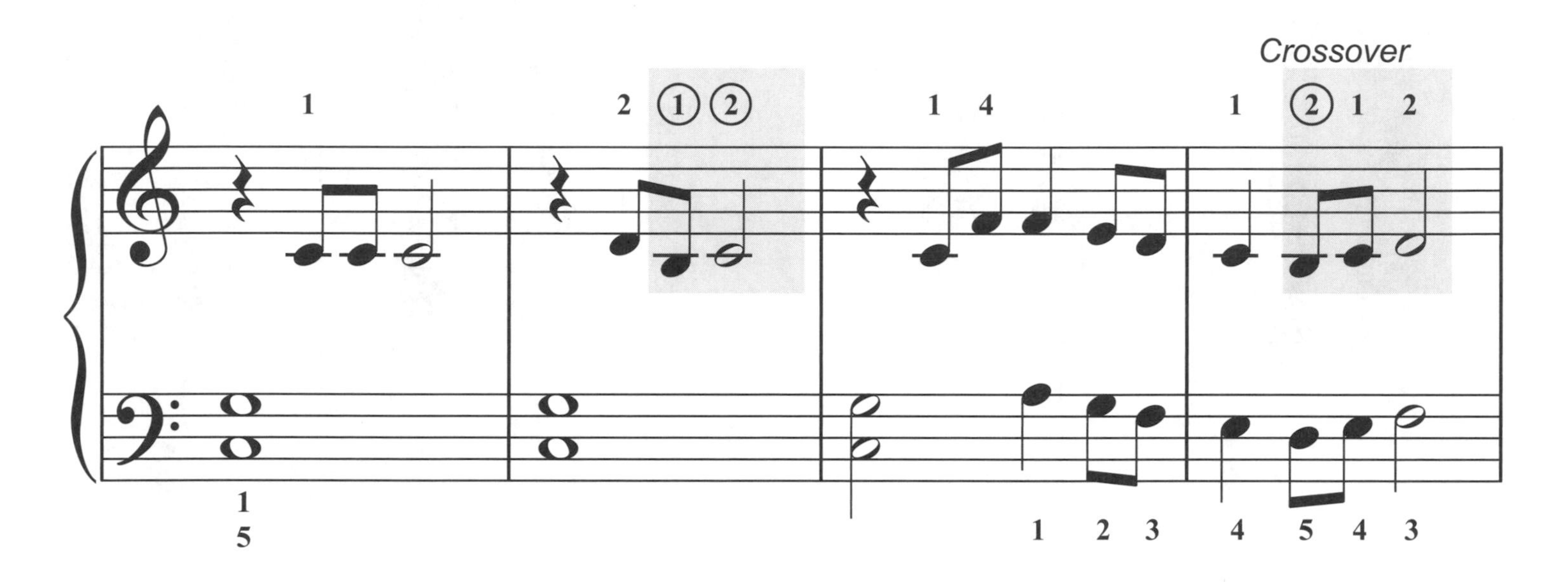

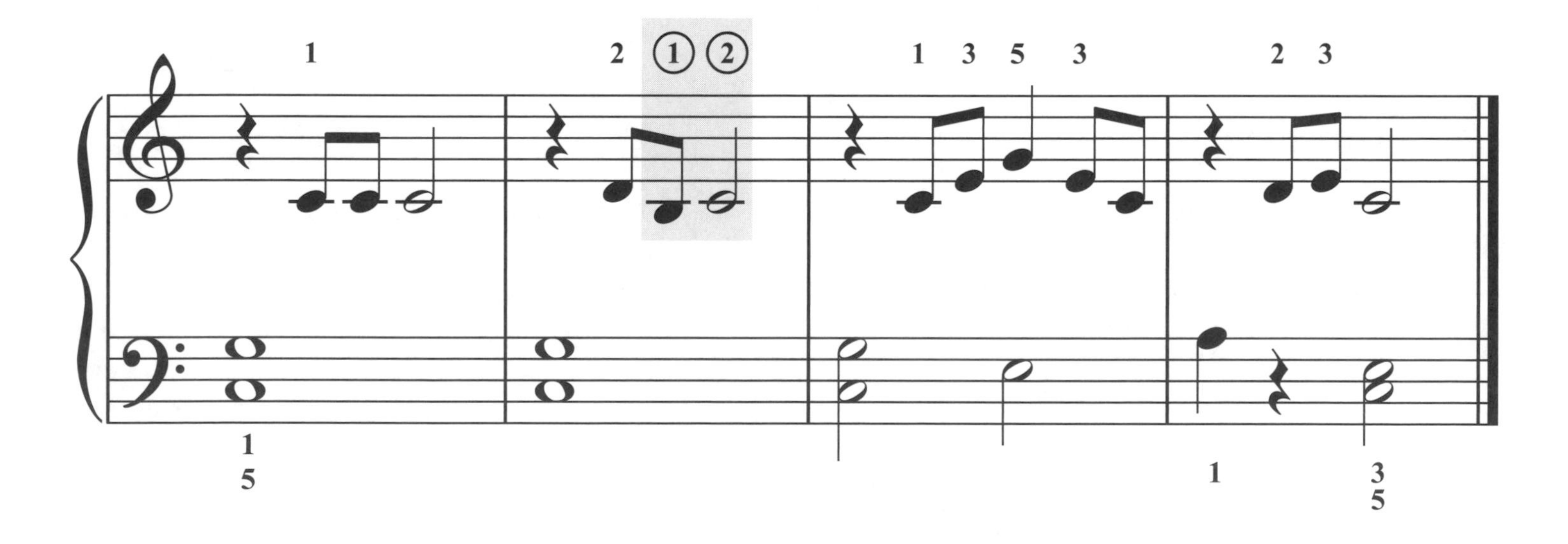

Learn Piano 2 - Quiz 1

Once you complete this section go to RockHouseSchool.com and take the quiz to track your progress. You will receive an email with your results and suggestions.

Your First Chords

CD Track 31-32

C Major

A chord is three or more notes sounded together. A major chord has a happy, bright sound. There is an easy way to form a major chord which I call the 4-3 method. By counting up four keys, then three keys, from any note you form a major chord. This is also four half steps and three half steps. Let's form a C major chord:

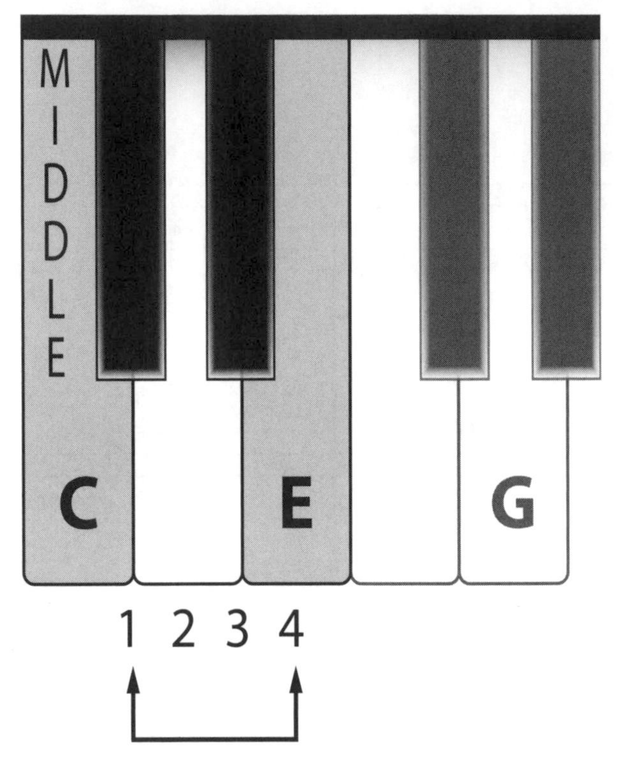

Start with the middle C note (the starting note is the root note, or name, of the chord), count up four keys (both black and white) this is the E note.

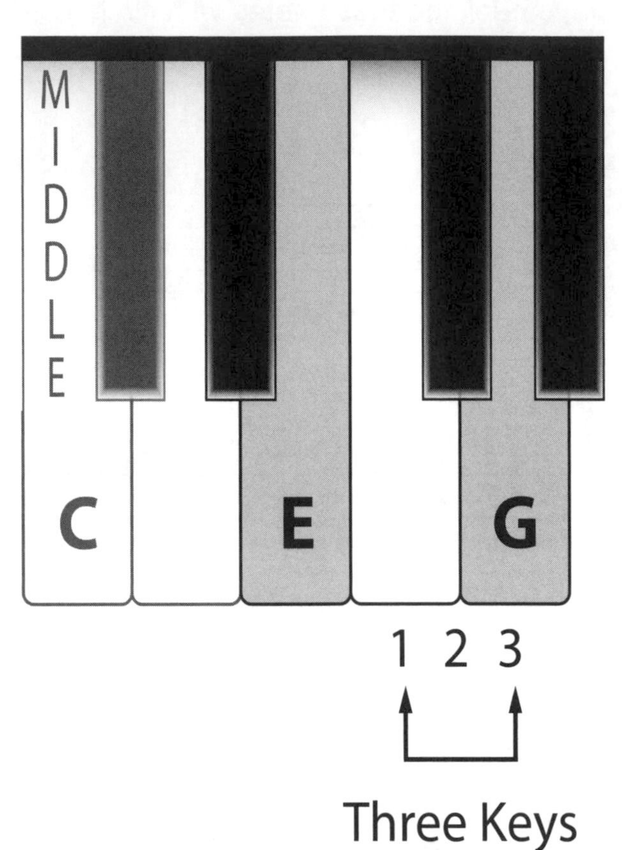

Next count up three keys, this is the G note.

The C major chord contains the notes C – E – G played together. Make sure to use the proper fingers to play the chord most effectively.

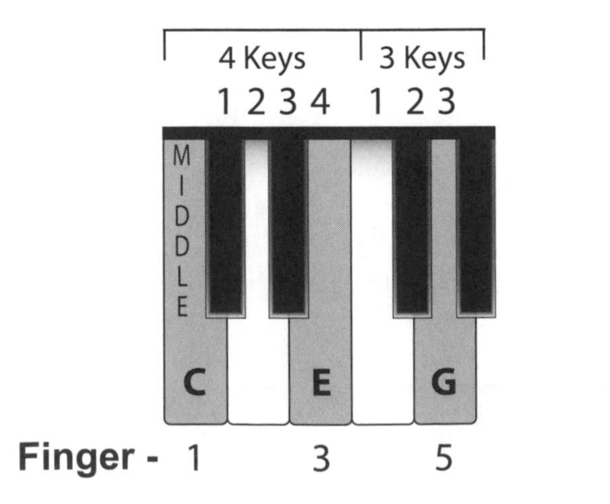

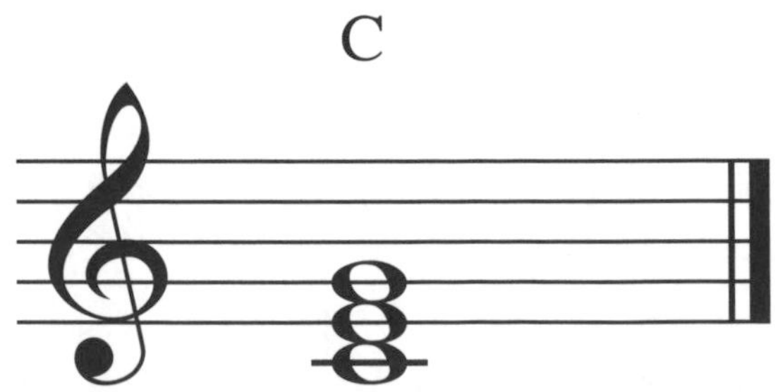

F Major

Now use the same method to form an F major chord. Start with the F note and go four keys up, this is the A note. Next go up three keys, this is the C note. The F major chord contains the notes F – A – C played together. Again, make sure to use the proper fingers to play each note.

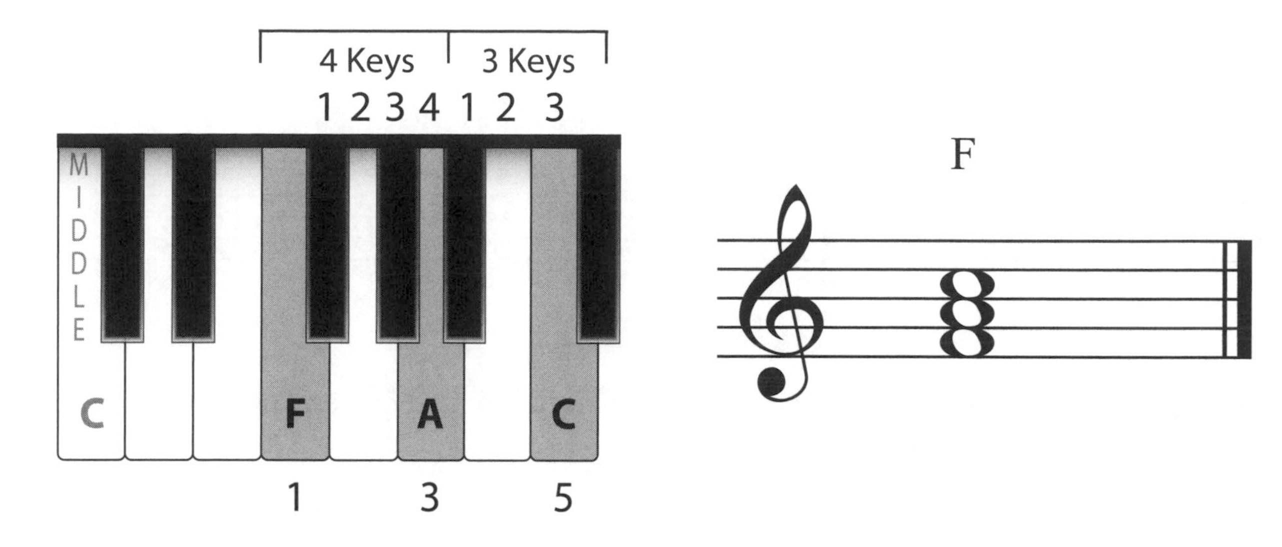

Playing Chords Across the Keyboard

You can play these two chords anywhere on the piano's keyboard. Play each chord starting with the lowest notes up to the highest. The keyboard diagrams below show where these chords are found across the piano.

C Major

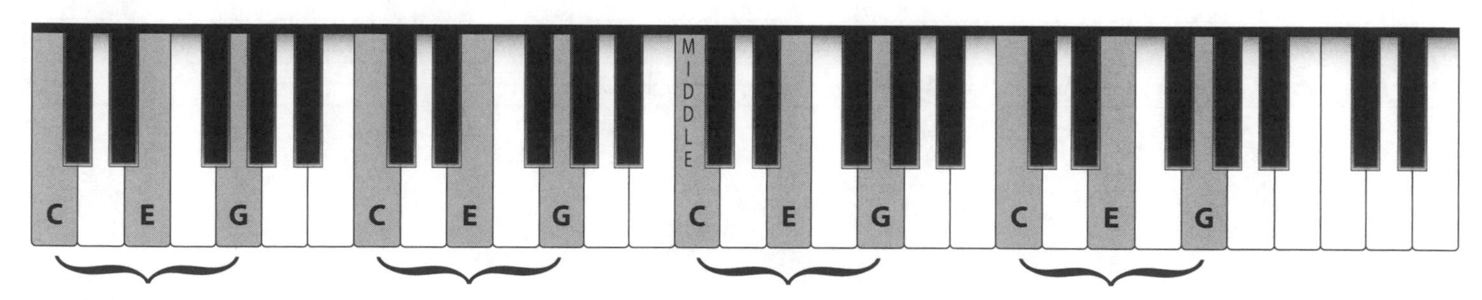

F Major

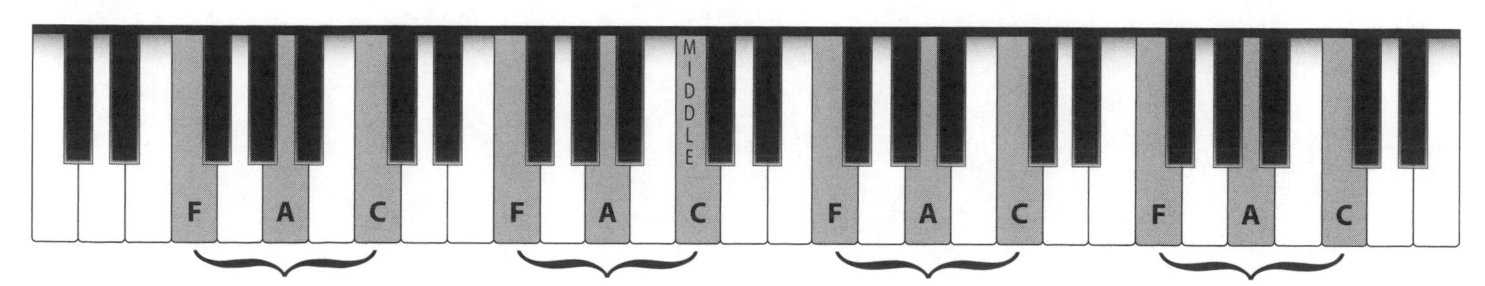

Your First Chord Progression

Now you will play the C and F major chords and form your first chord progression. Play each chord two times in whole note timing. Play the chord progression below along with the backing track and hear how it makes a complete song.

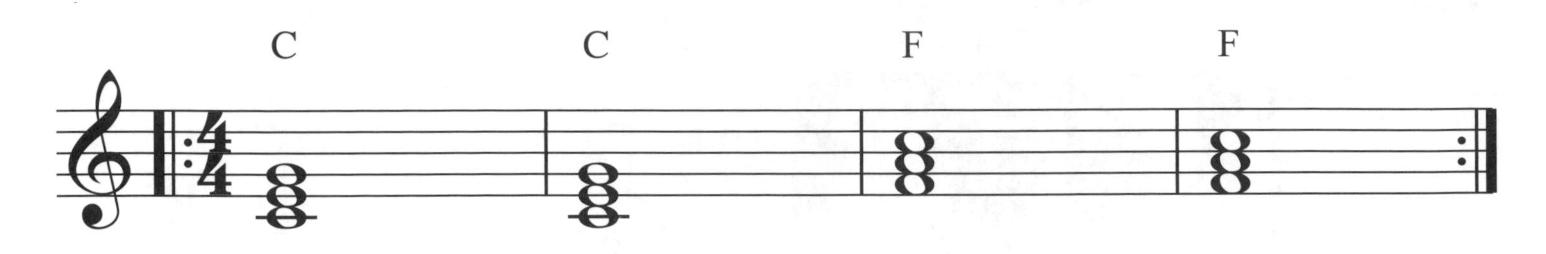

You can play the same chord progression with half and quarter note timing. Play the progressions below. You can also play these variations along with the same backing track.

Half Notes

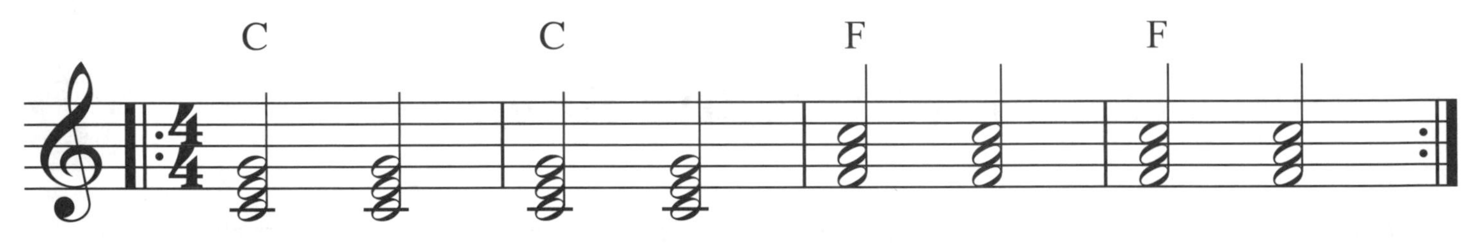

Quarter Notes

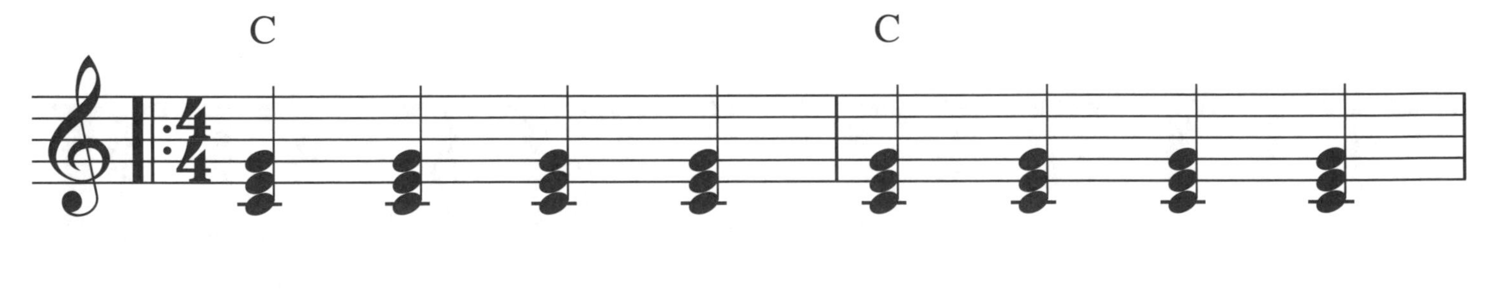

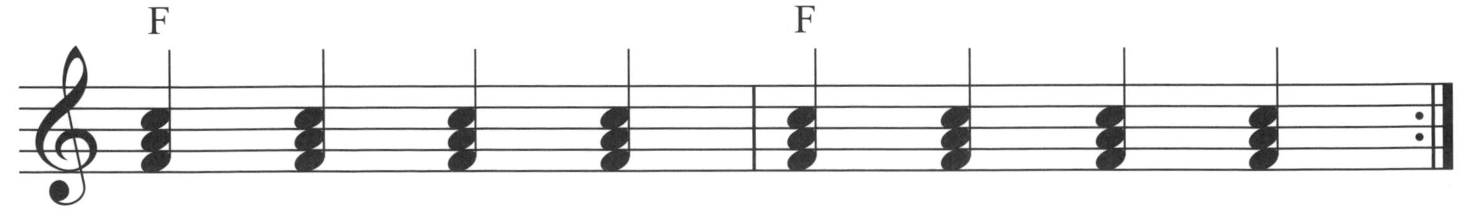

Sustain & Damper Pedal

Most pianos come with two or three pedals. The pedal on the far right is called the *damper* pedal. Many times this pedal is also called a sustain pedal. When the pedal is pressed it "turns on" the sustained effect by lifting the dampers off of the piano strings which allows the notes to ring even after you have lifted your fingers away from the keys. If you are using an electric keyboard most have an input for a sustain pedal to plug in on the back.

There are very specific symbols used in classical music indicating when to press the sustain pedal and when the sustain should be off completely. The symbols look like this:

- Press down or change damper (sustain) pedal.

- Completely remove damper (sustain) pedal.

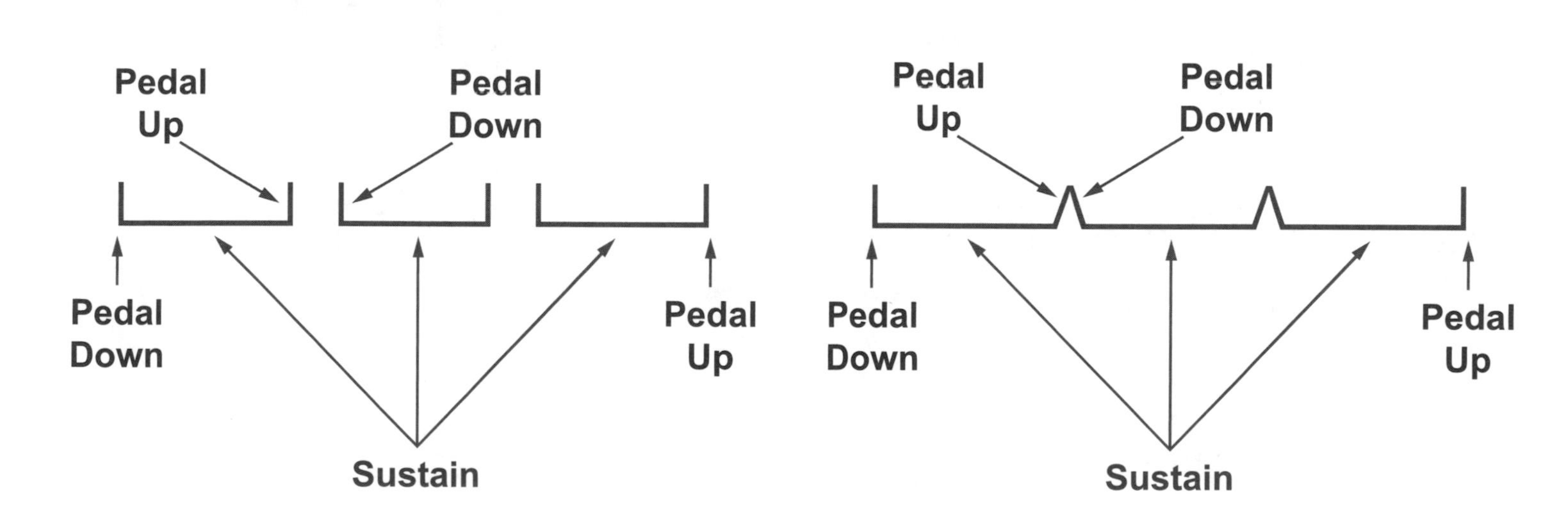

Below is an example of using the damper pedal in a musical context:

One last thing I want to mention; sometimes in popular music arrangements specific pedal symbols are not used. Instead, the words "with pedal" might be seen under the first measure. And in other cases there is no mention of the pedal leaving the usage of the pedal up to the performer. Use your discretion as well as your ears and you will always sound great when you play!

Single Note Exercises

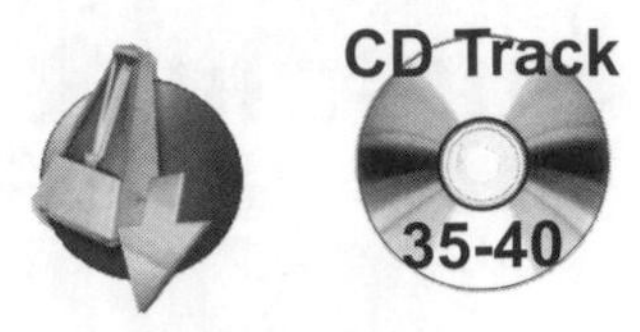

It is important to get your hands coordinated so you can play complicated pieces with ease. The following exercises will challenge your right and left hands. Take your time starting slowly then build your speed up gradually. I recommend that you use a metronome to help gauge your progress.

Example 1: Right Hand Ascending

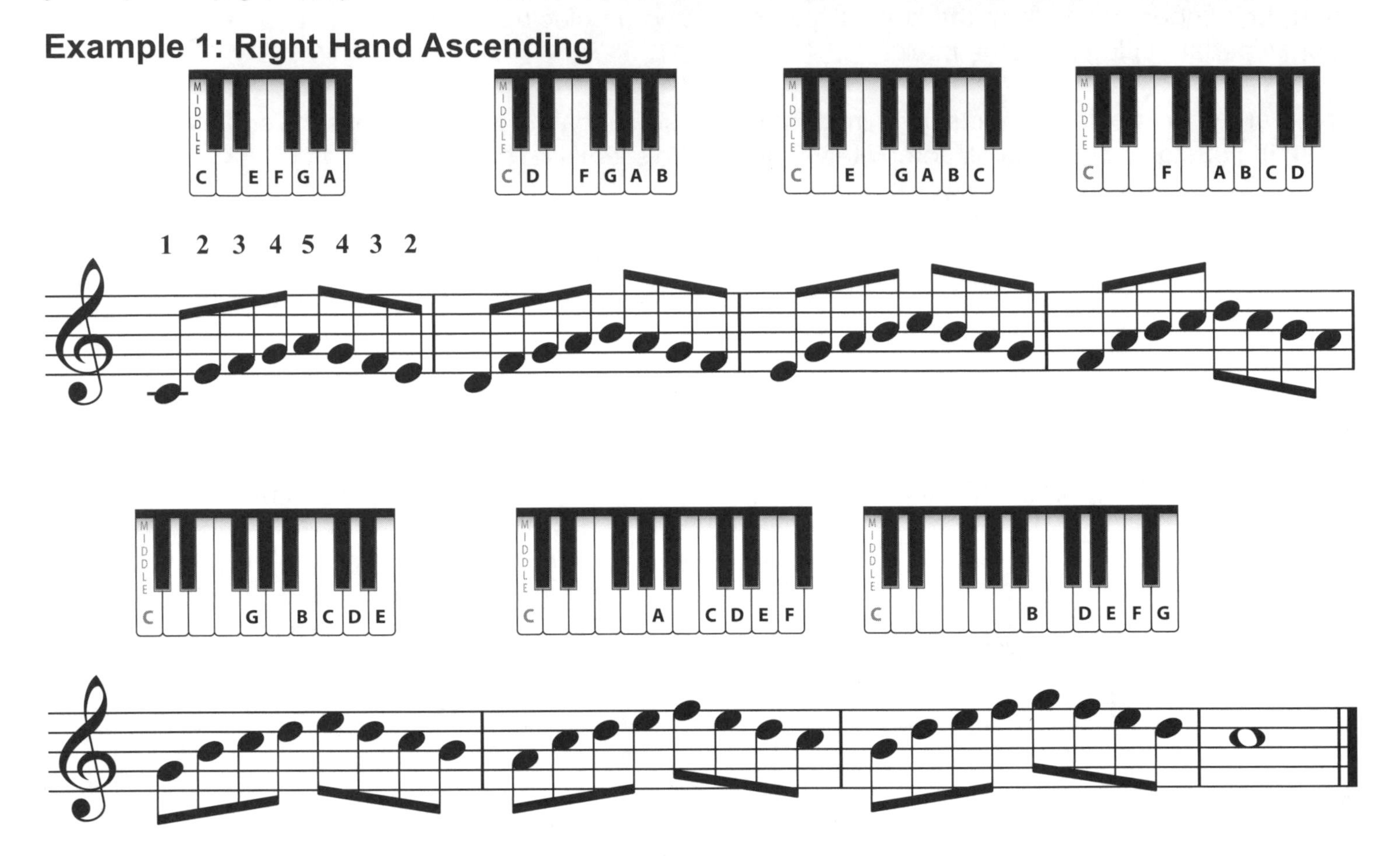

Right Hand Descending

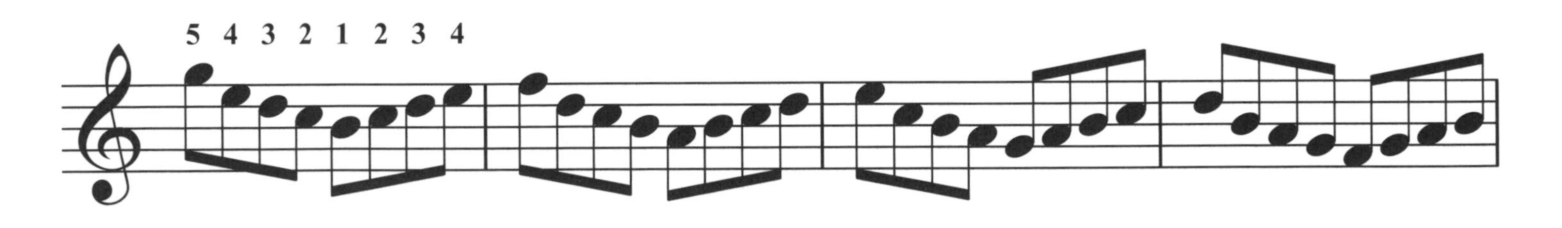

Example 2: Left Hand Ascending

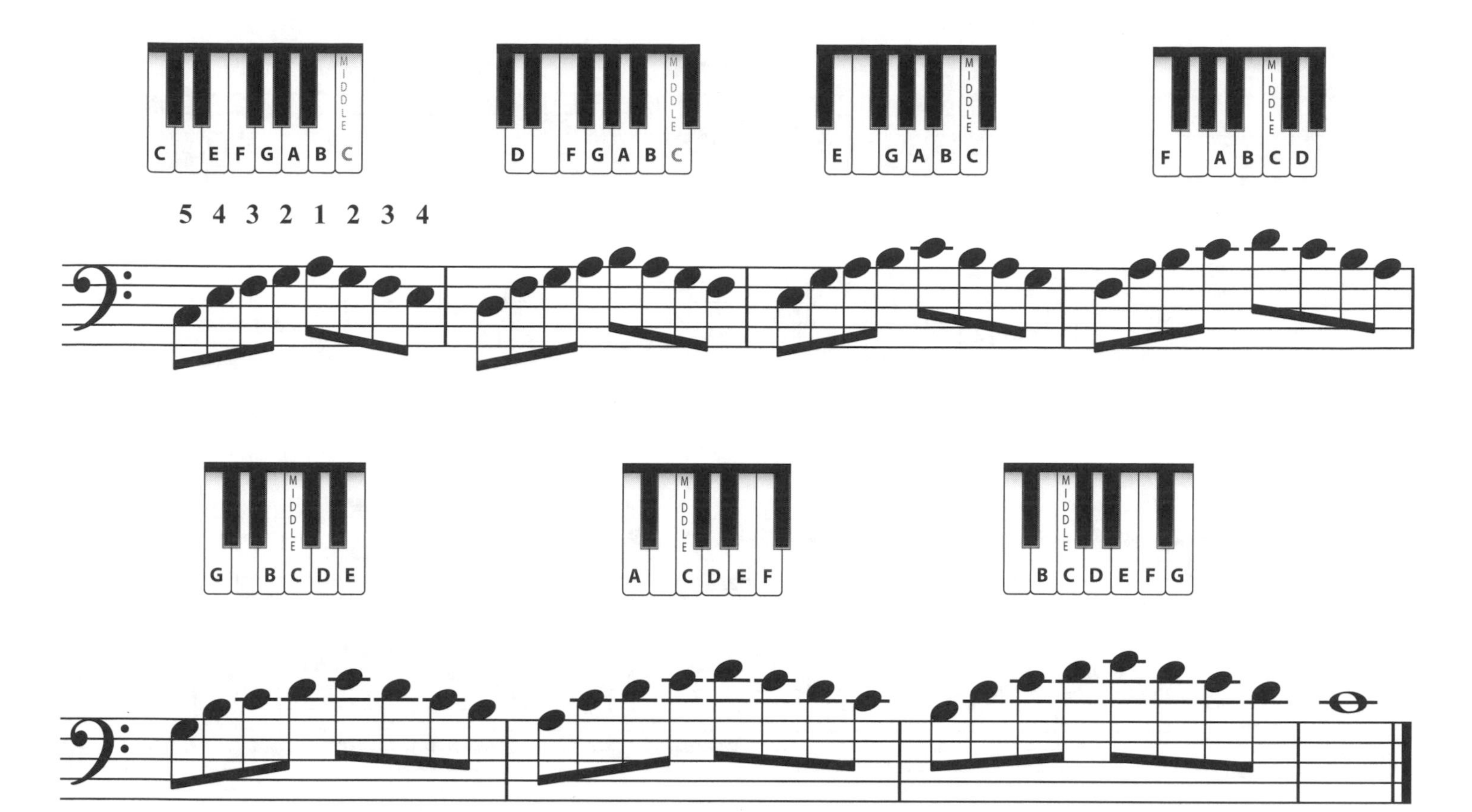

Left Hand Descending

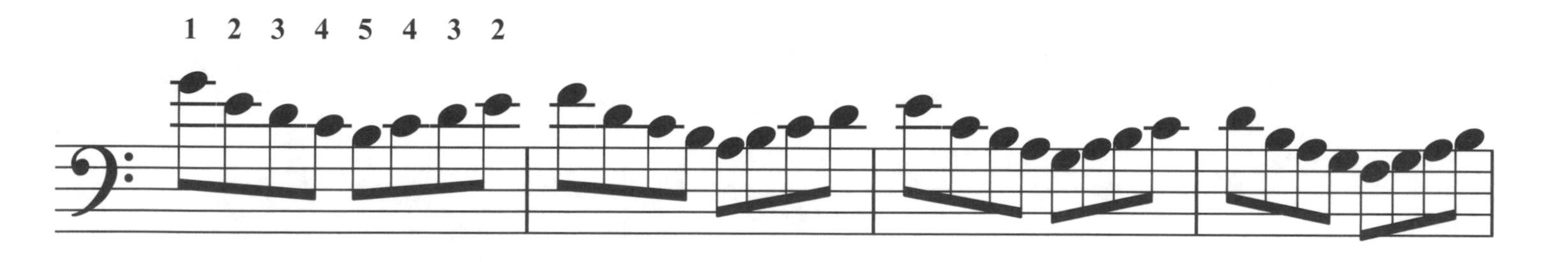

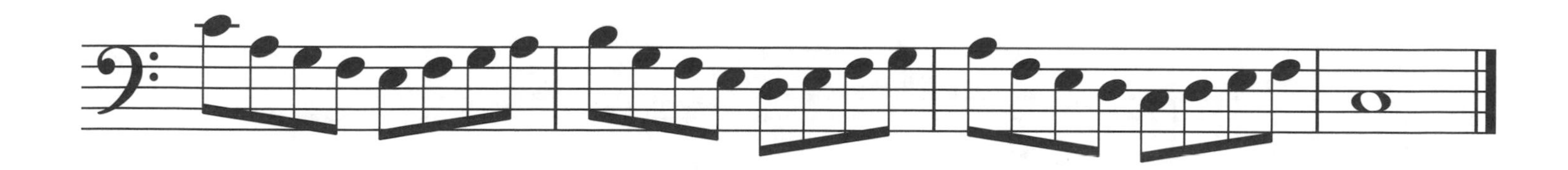

Example 3: Both Hands Ascending

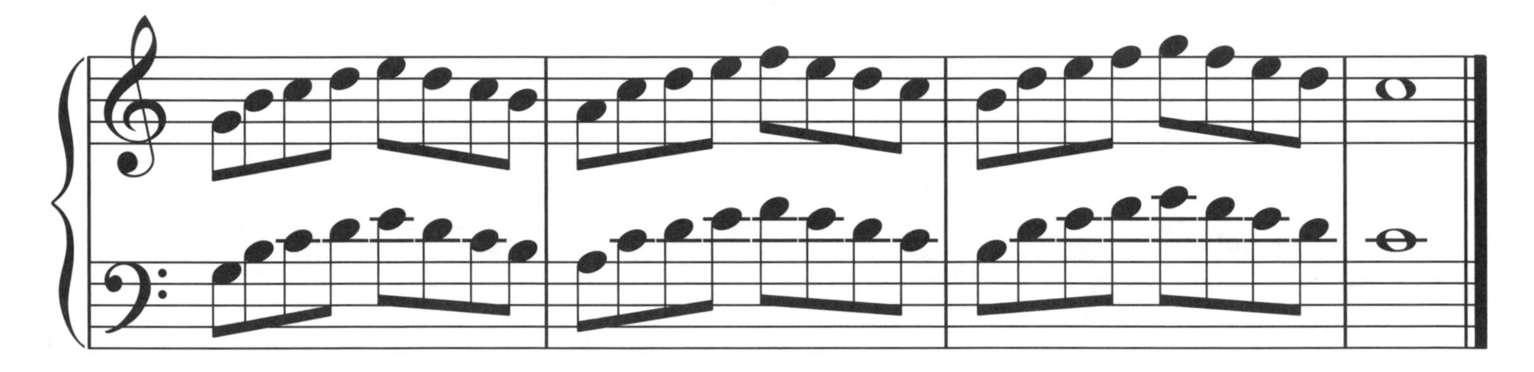

Both Hands Descending

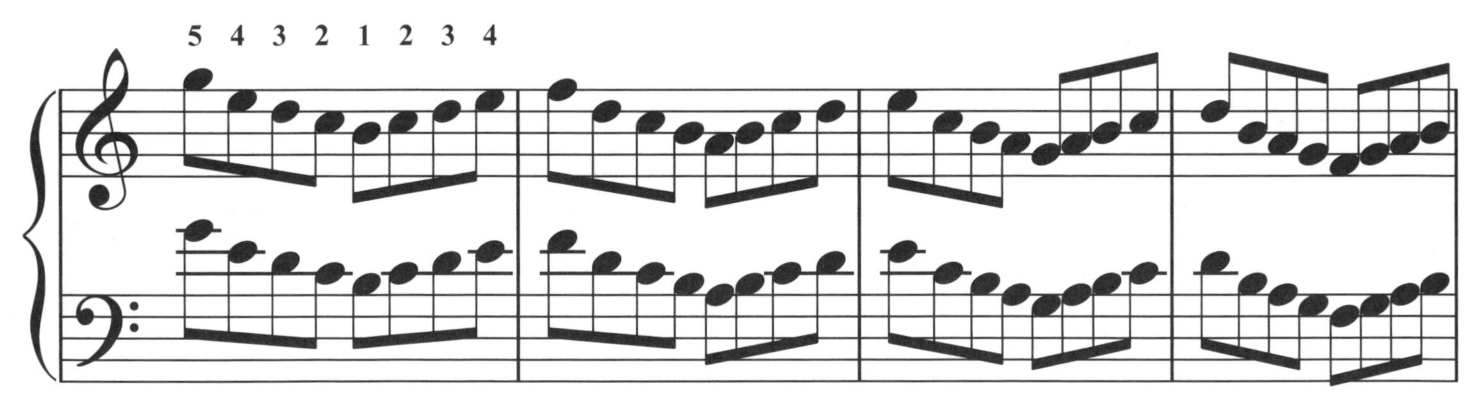

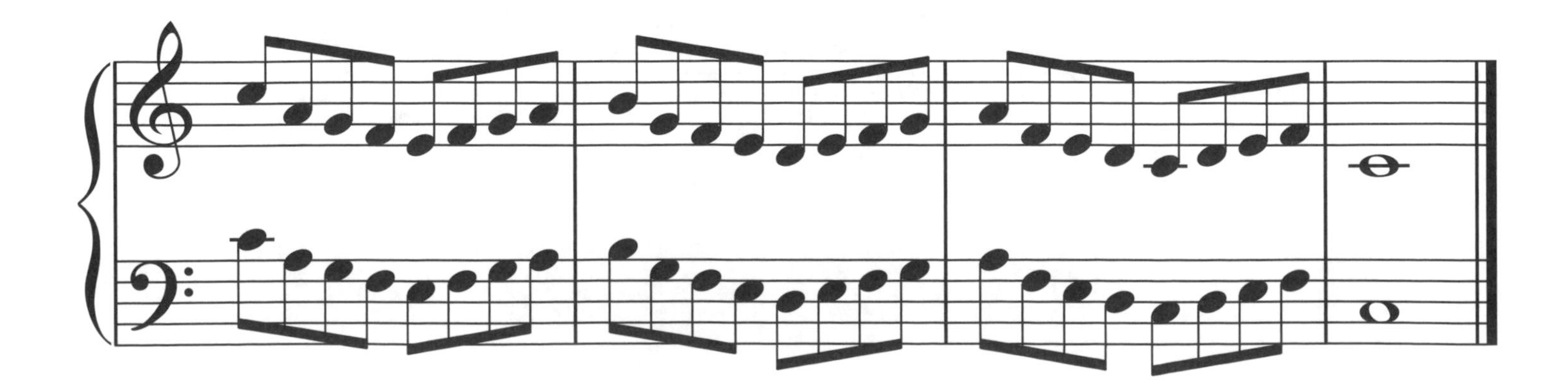

Intervals – Whole & Half Steps

As you learned earlier, if you play any note and then play the next key you are playing a half step. There are two natural half steps that are B to C and E to F. These are two white keys in a row. A whole step is made up of two half steps.

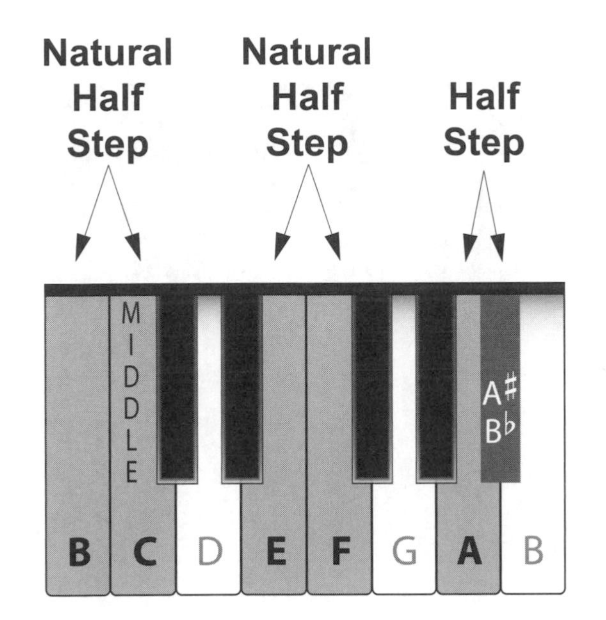

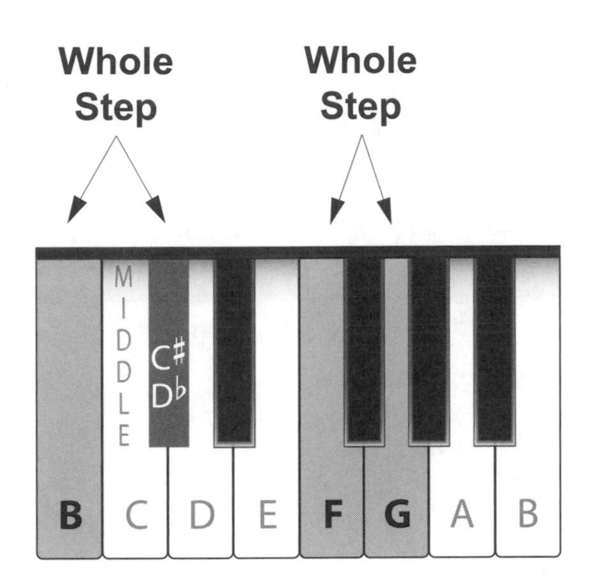

Writing Half & Whole Steps

Now that you have learned what a half and whole step are on the keyboard write a series of half and whole steps on the keyboard diagrams below. Write the letter name of the two notes directly on the key and over the diagram write an H or W for whole or half step. I've done a few to help you get started:

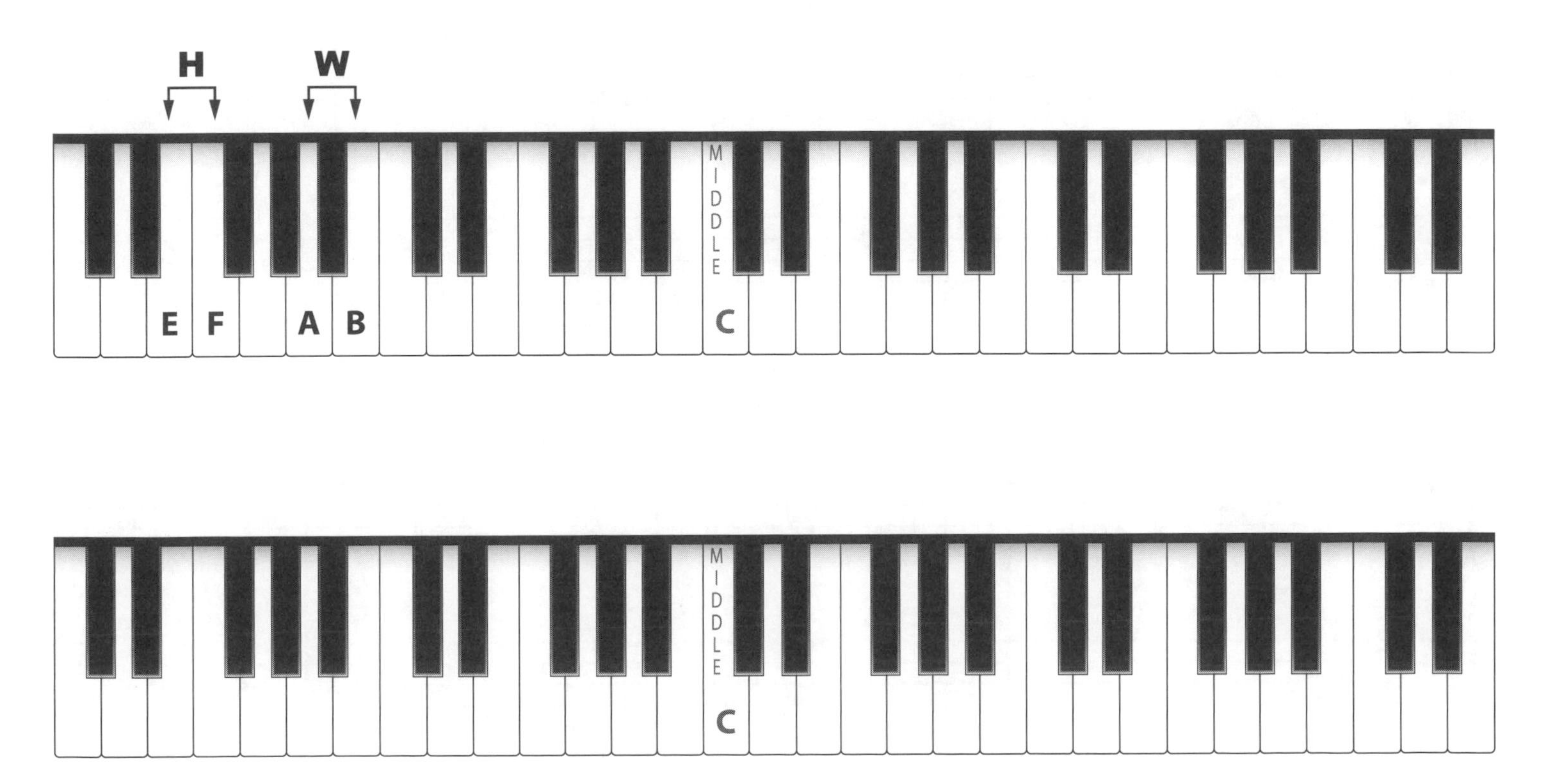

Intervals - 2nds

On the piano's keyboard, the interval from one white key to the next adjacent white key is a 2nd. When played in a row they are considered melodic 2nd intervals. If played together they would be harmonic 2nd intervals. A 2nd in music notation will be from line to the next space; or, space to the next line. As you progress you must train your ear to hear different intervals so you can learn and write your own music effectively. Play the following 2nd intervals and make sure to hear their unique sound.

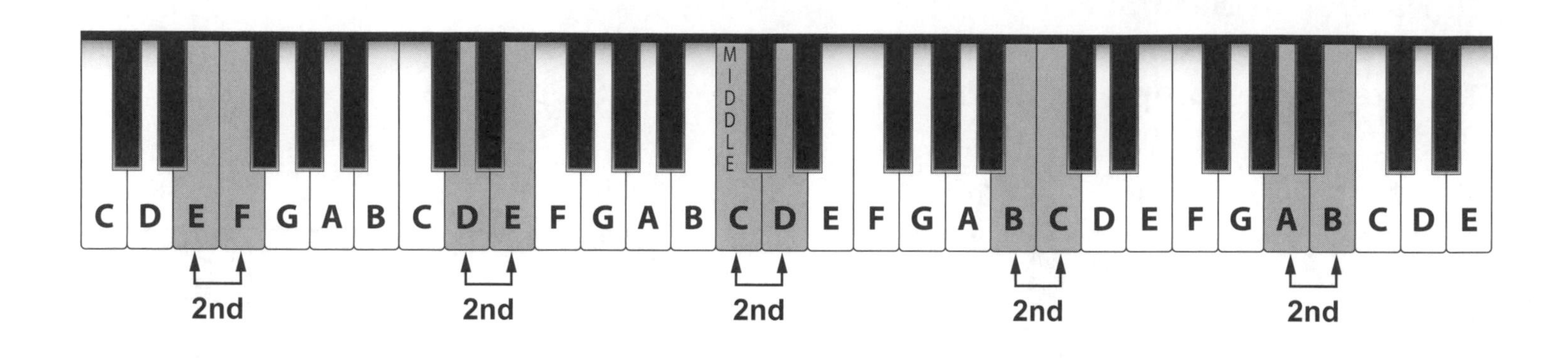

2nds Etude

Here is an etude that has many 2nd intervals included. See if you can locate all the 2nds within this piece. The coordination between both hands may be difficult in the beginning. Try each hand separately first, then put them both together.

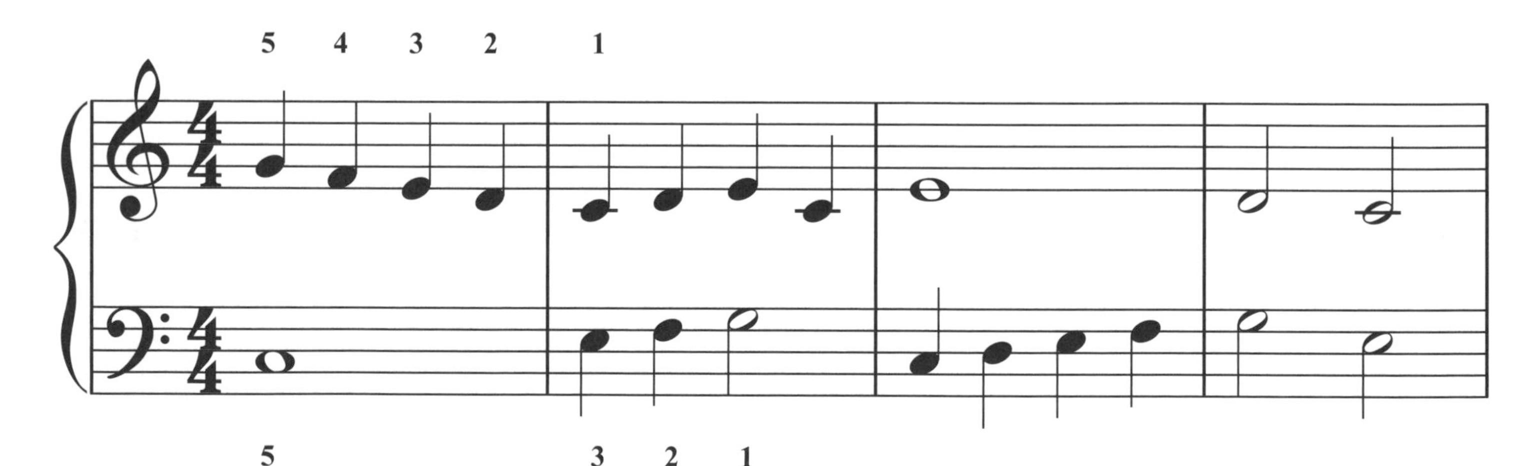

Intervals - 3rds

On the keyboard a 3rd interval is two white keys away from any white key. A 3rd interval in music notation is from any line or space to the next. If there are three keys up to the second note it will be a minor 3rd, if there are four keys it is a major 3rd. Play the notes in a row and you can hear that the major 3rd sounds happy while the minor 3rd sounds sad. Again make sure to listen to the 3rd interval and hear its unique sound. Play the examples below:

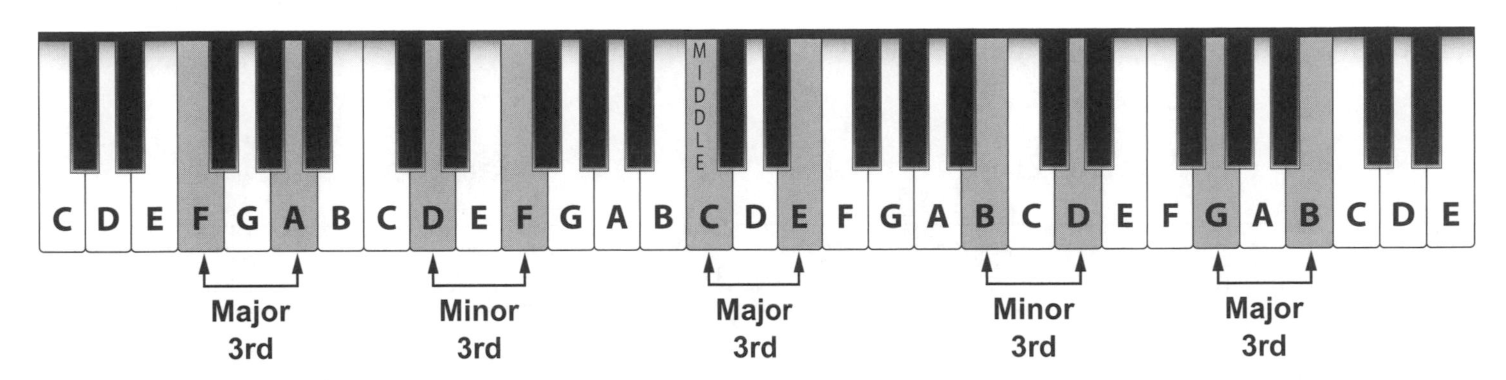

3rds Etude

Here is an etude that has many 3rd intervals included. See if you can locate all the 3rds within this piece.

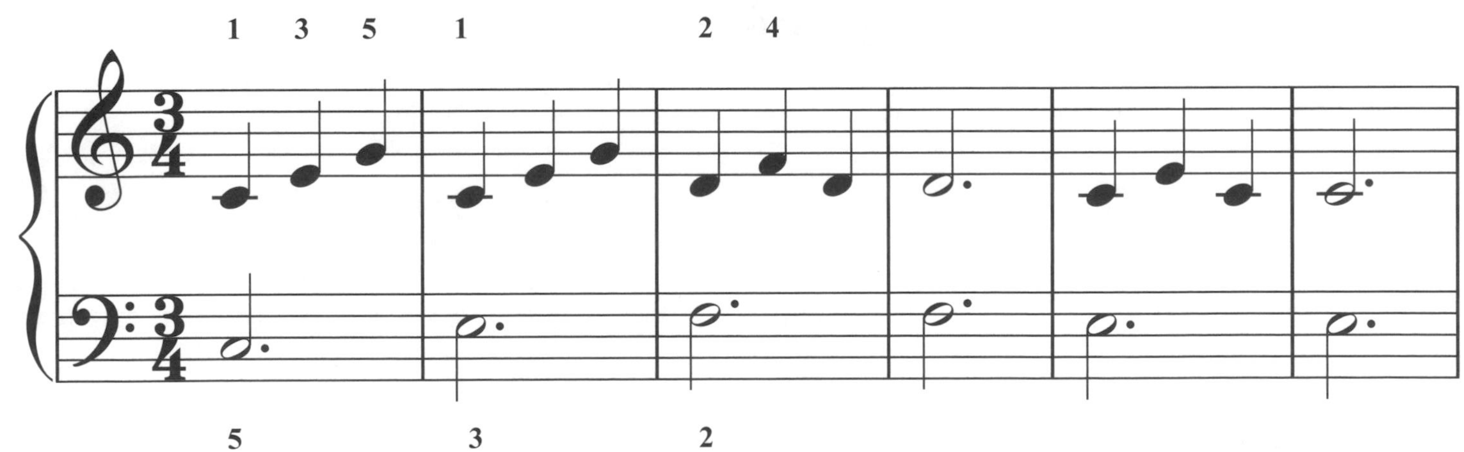

Seeing Intervals

An important thing to note: in music notation all even numbered intervals, such as 2nds or 4ths will always go from a line to space or space to line. In turn, all odd number intervals like 3rds or 5ths will always go from line to line or space to space. If the intervals are played in a row they are called melodic intervals, if played together they are called harmonic intervals. Play the 2nd and 3rd intervals below and connect the way they look with their sound.

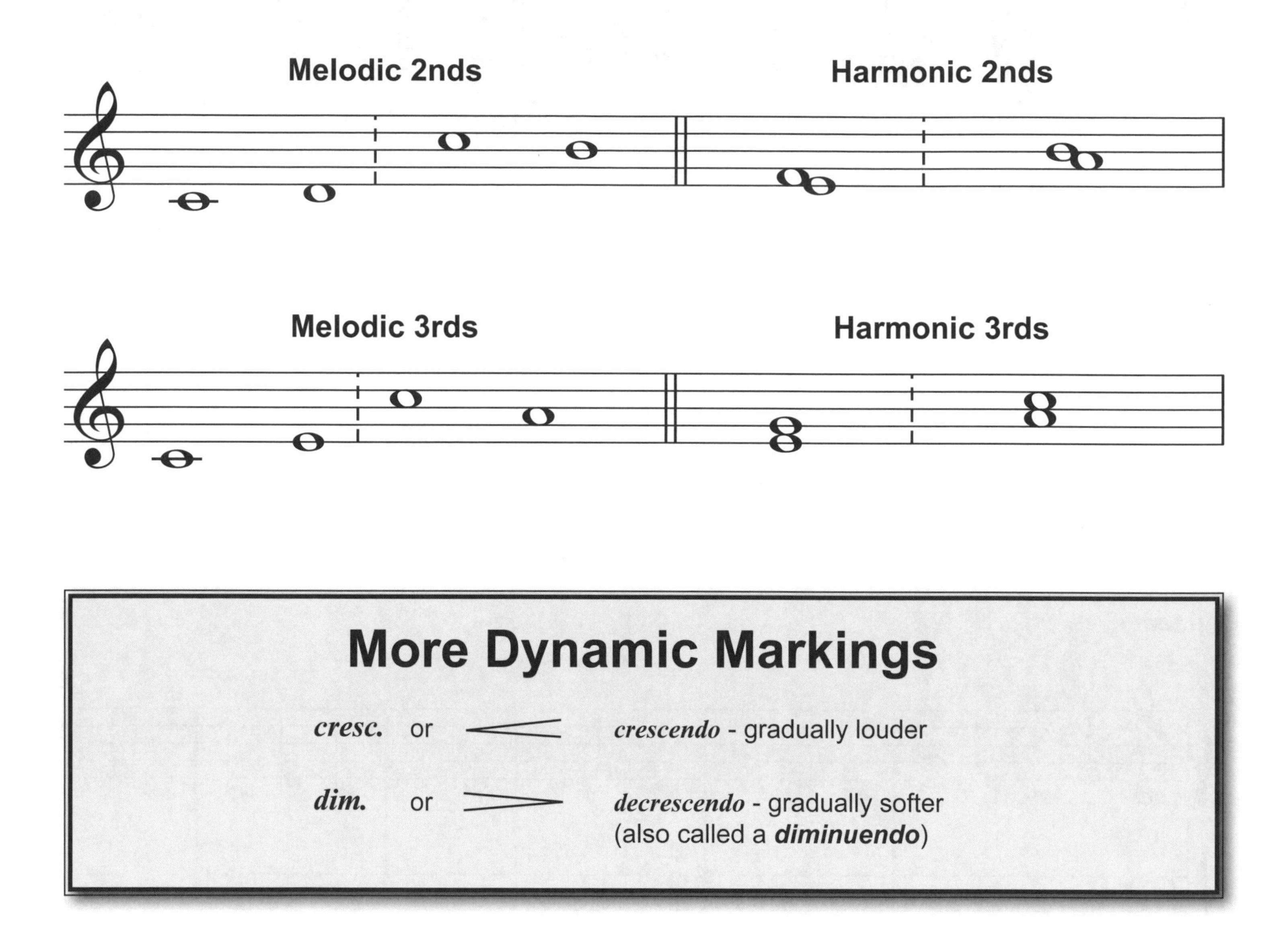

Alternate Fingerings

In the next two songs there will be alternate fingerings that you will use. I have depicted these fingerings with circles around them. In Brahms' "Lullaby" you will be extending the notes higher with your right hand. In "This Land is Your Land" you will extend the right hand lower using a cross over. Pay attention to these fingering to play these songs properly. You will be expanding your reach on the keyboard more and more as you progress.

Brahms' Lullaby

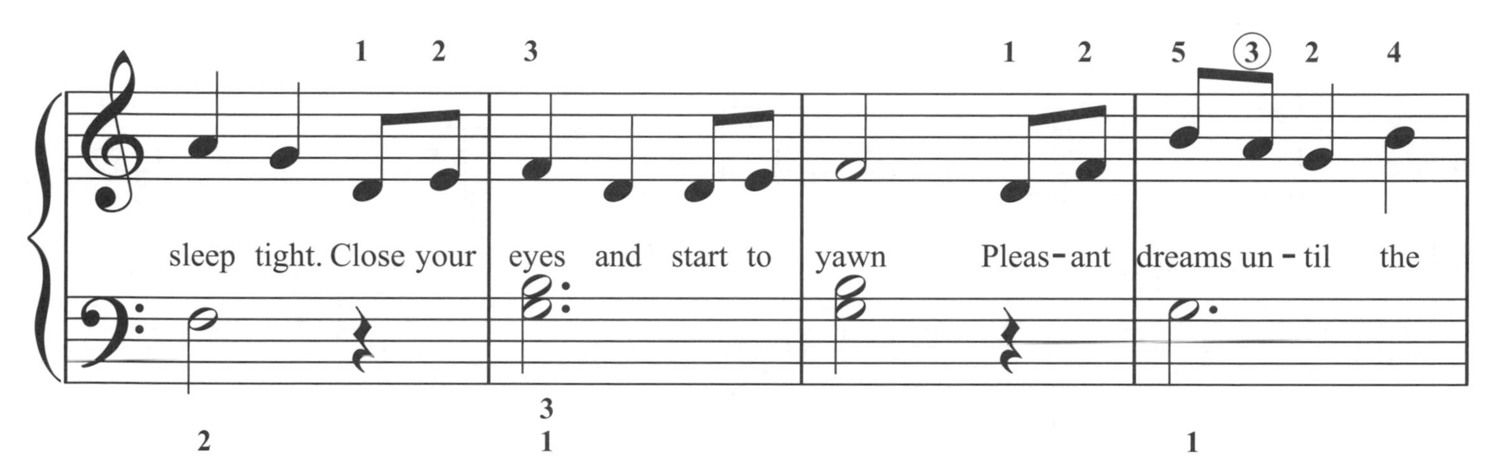

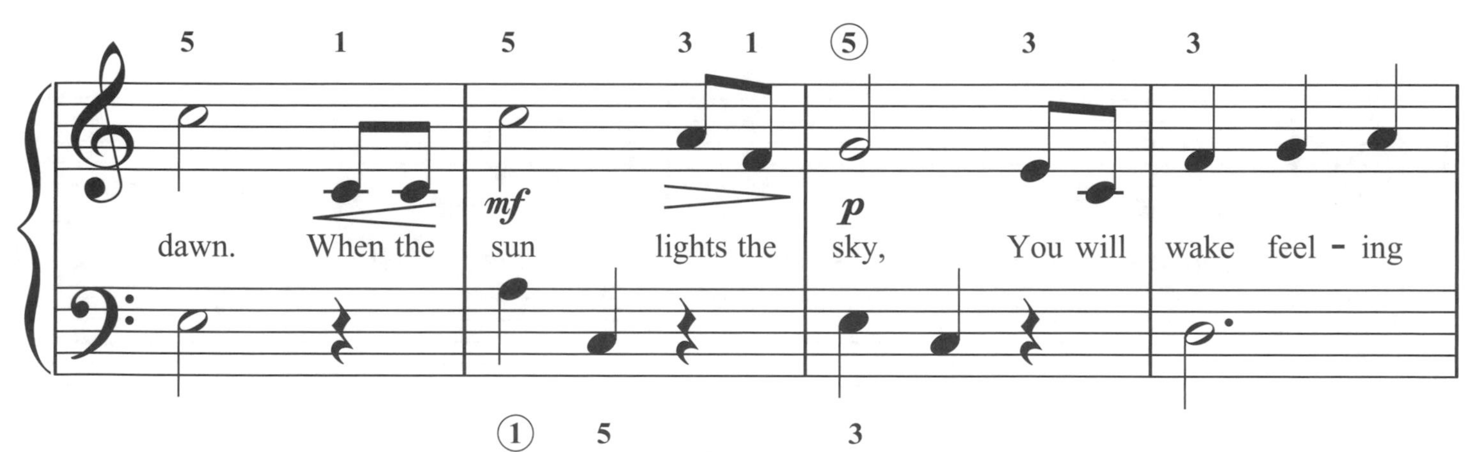

This Land is Your Land

CD Track 48-50

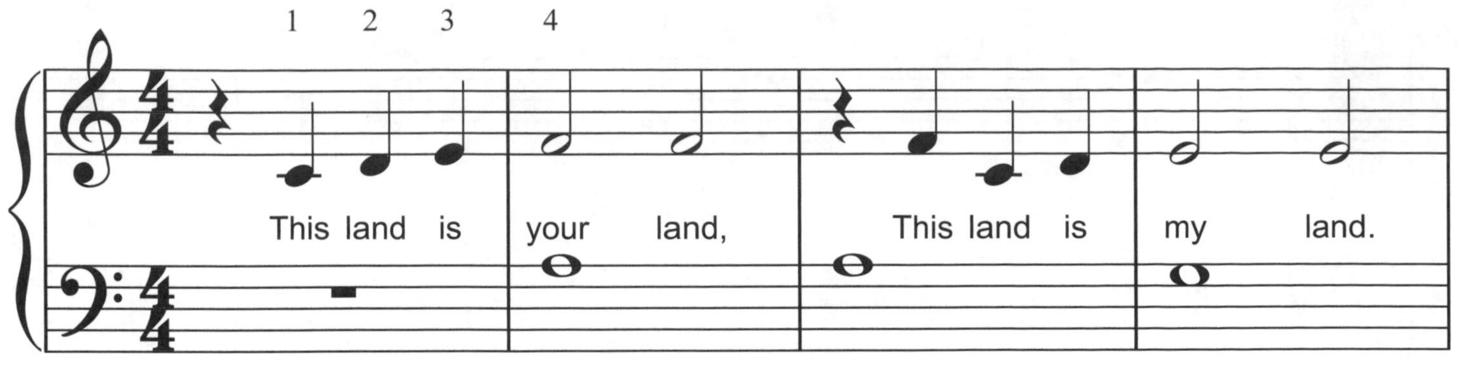

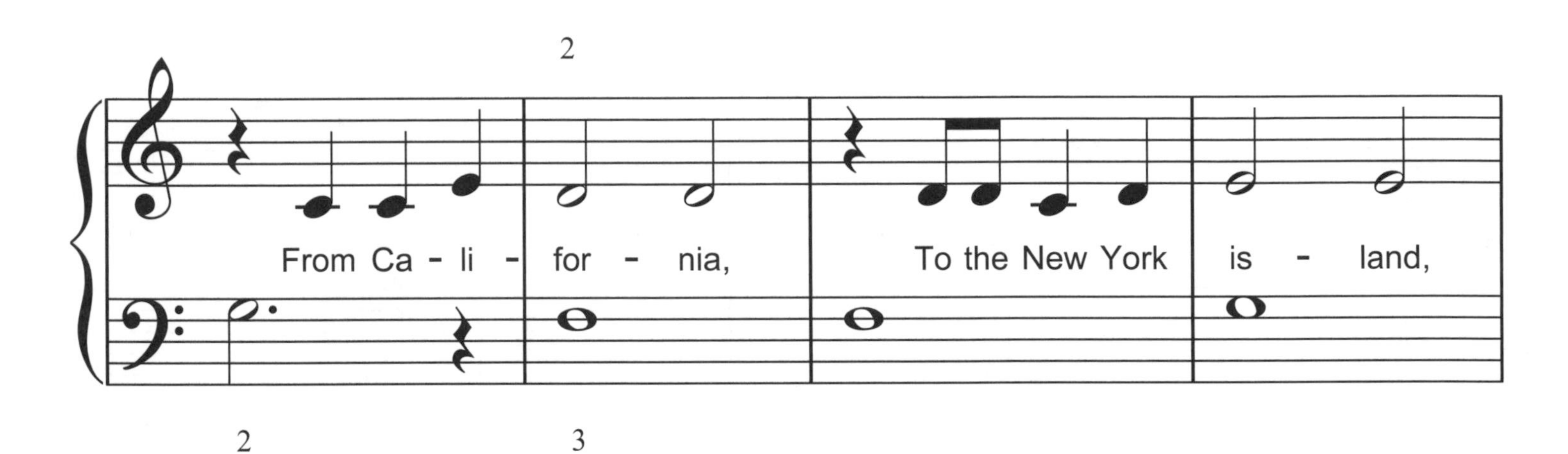

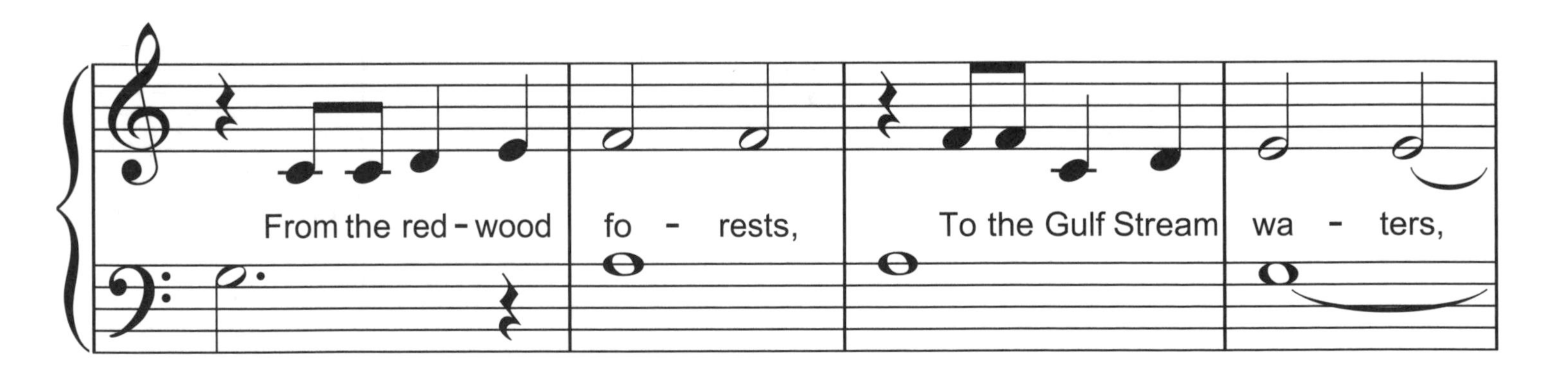

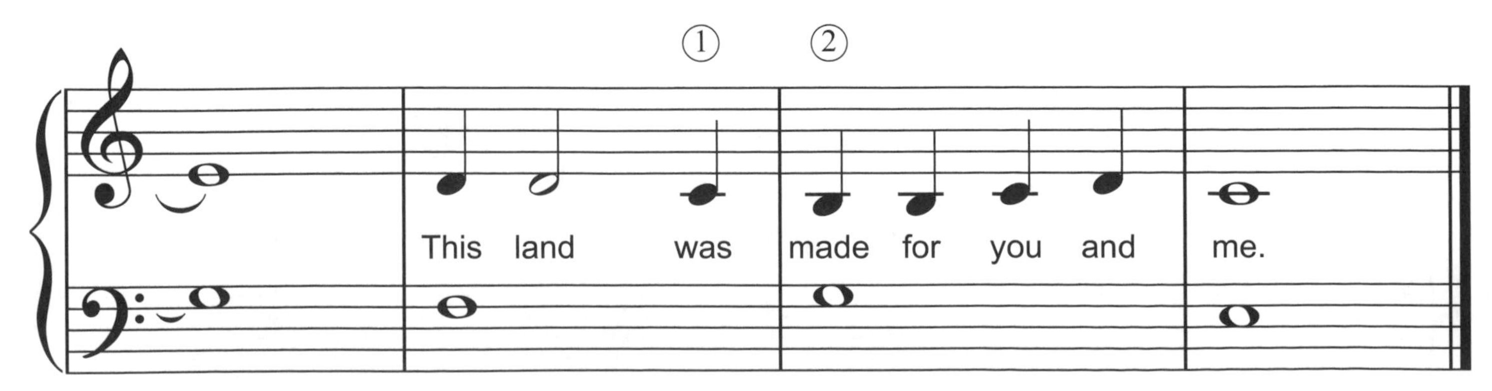

Intervals - 4ths & 5ths

W

Fourths

To play a 4th you skip two white keys.

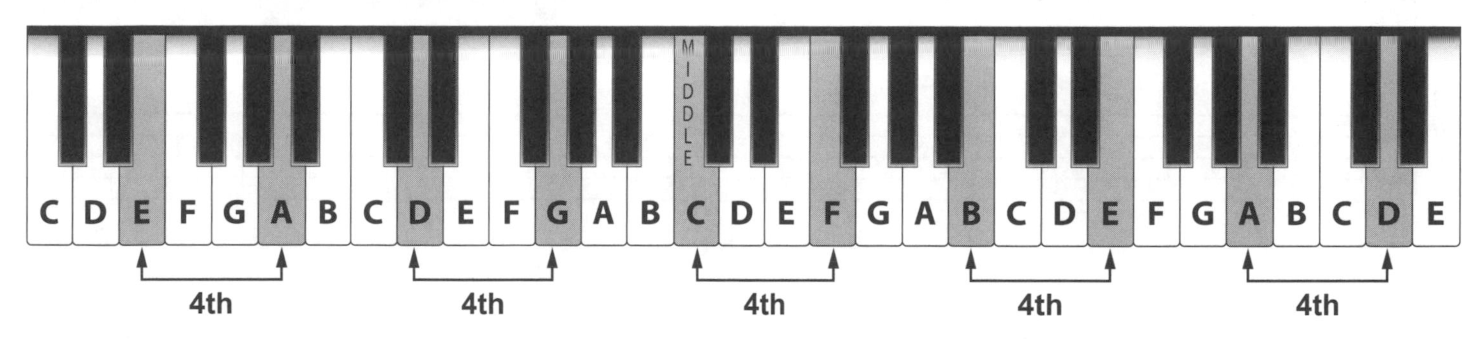

Fifths

To play a 5th you skip 3 white keys.

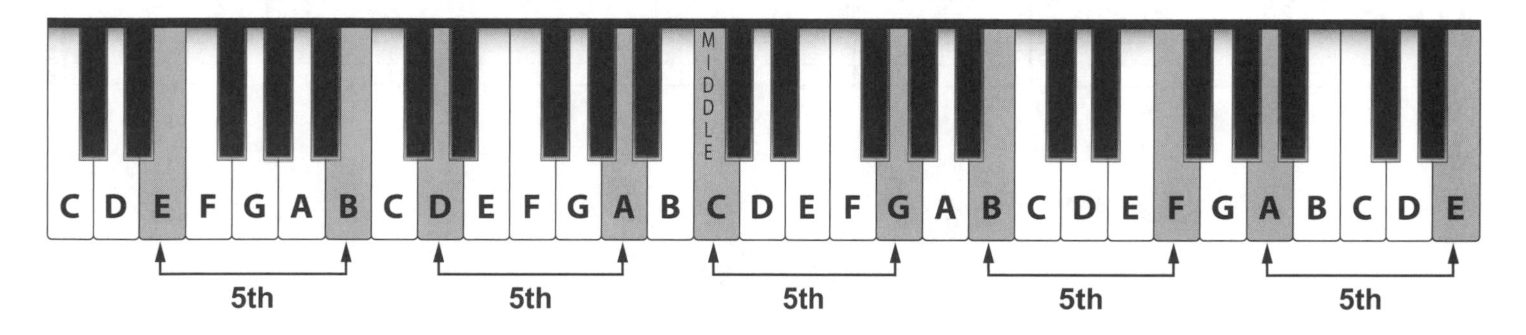

An important thing to remember, 4ths will always go from a line to space or space to line and 5ths will always go from line to line or space to space. Play the 4th and 5th intervals below and train your ears to hear their sound.

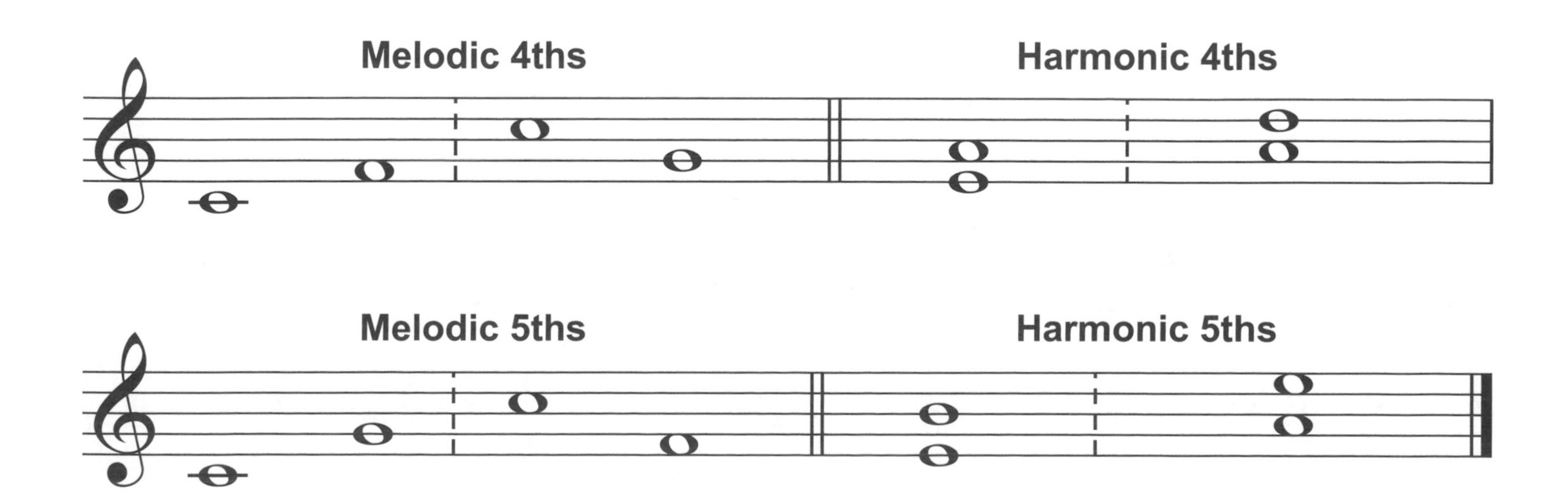

4ths Etude

Andante

5ths Etude

CD Track
53-54

Andante

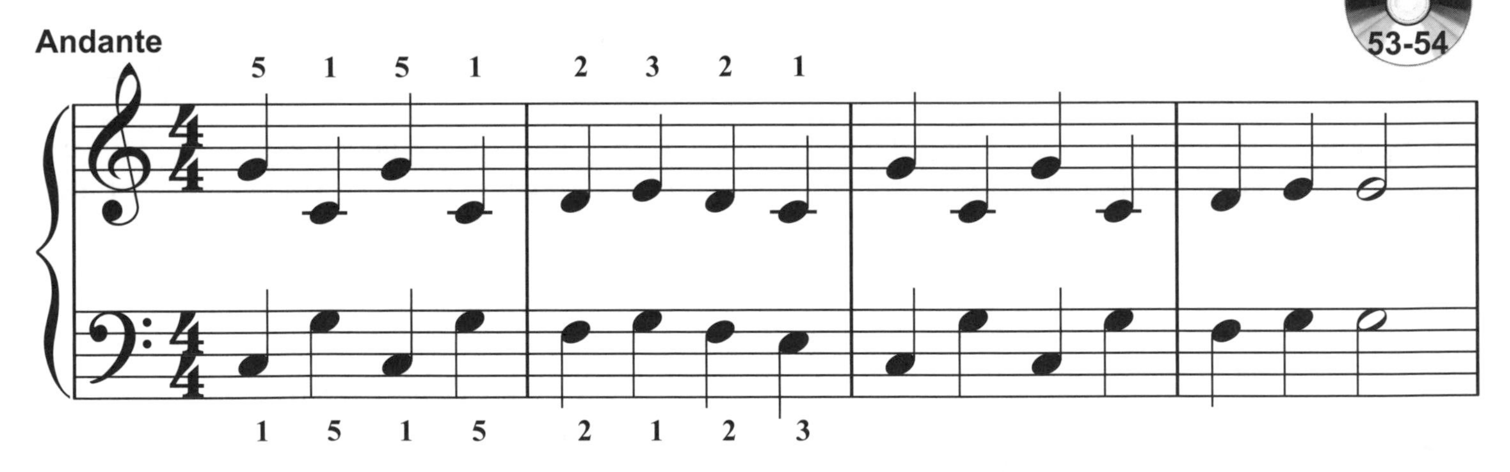

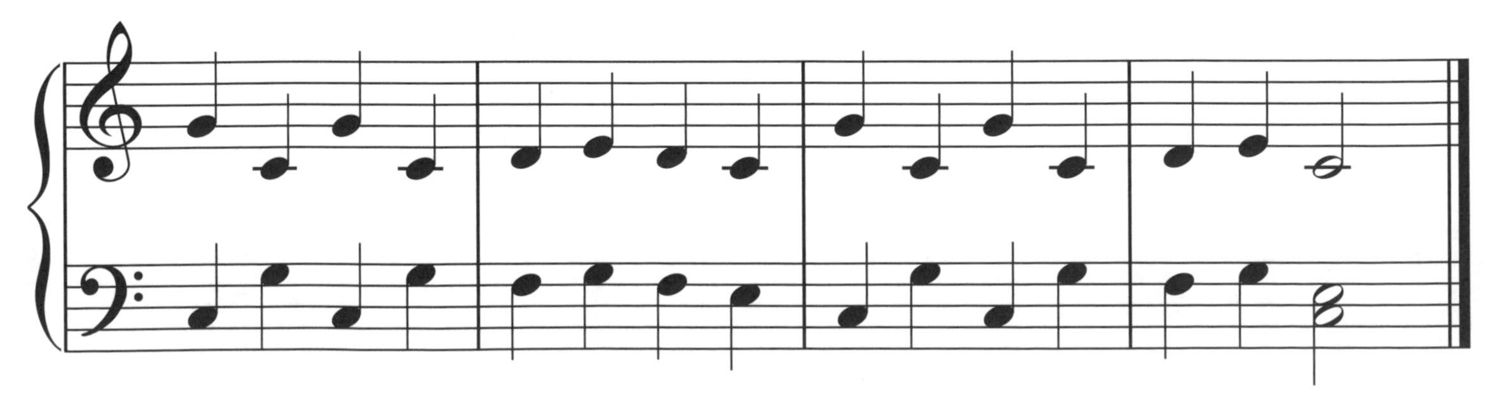

Oh! Susanna

In this song there is a C major chord played with the left hand. Notice how the C major chord is a 3rd and 5th interval together. Intervals are combined to create chords.

America (My Country Tis of Thee)

In this song you will find 2nd, 3rd and 5th intervals. Many times the left and right hand noted together form chords.

Andante

Kum-Ba-Ya

CD Track 60

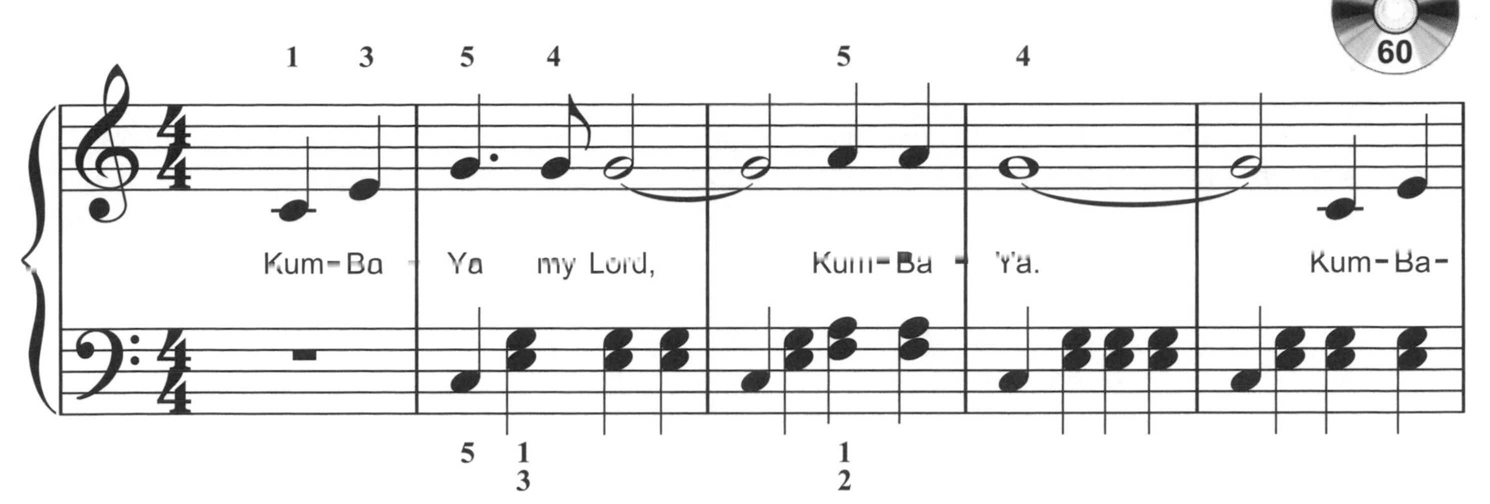

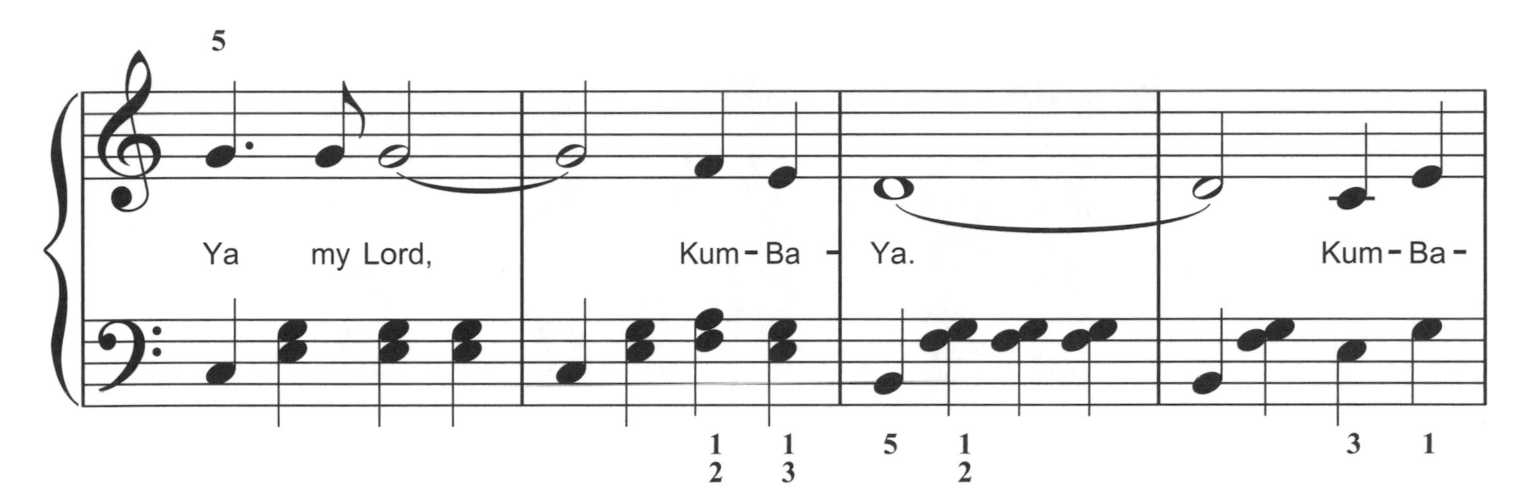

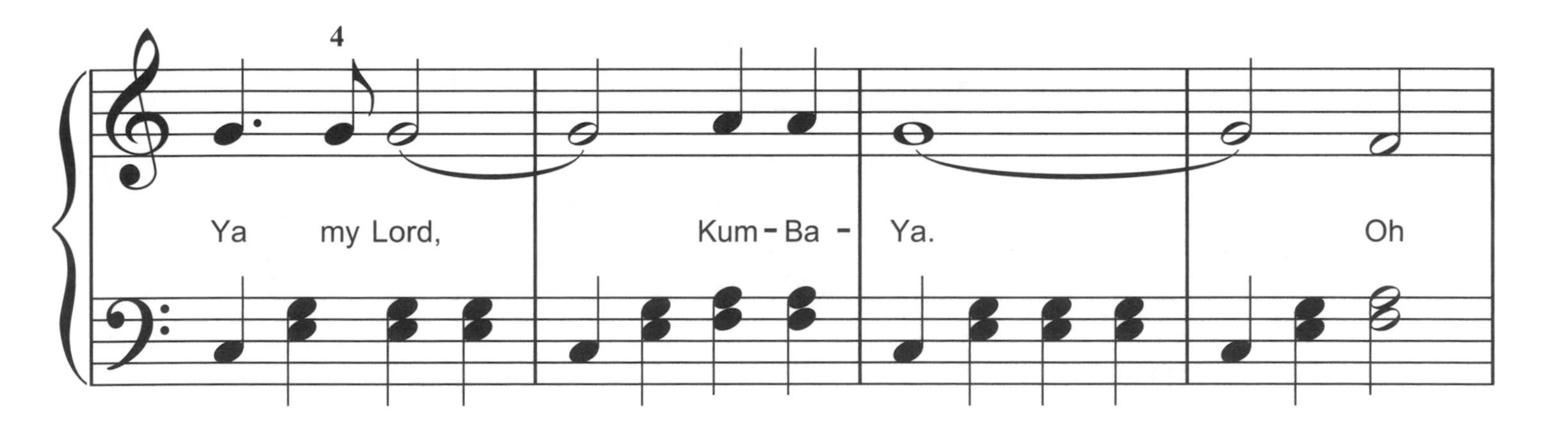

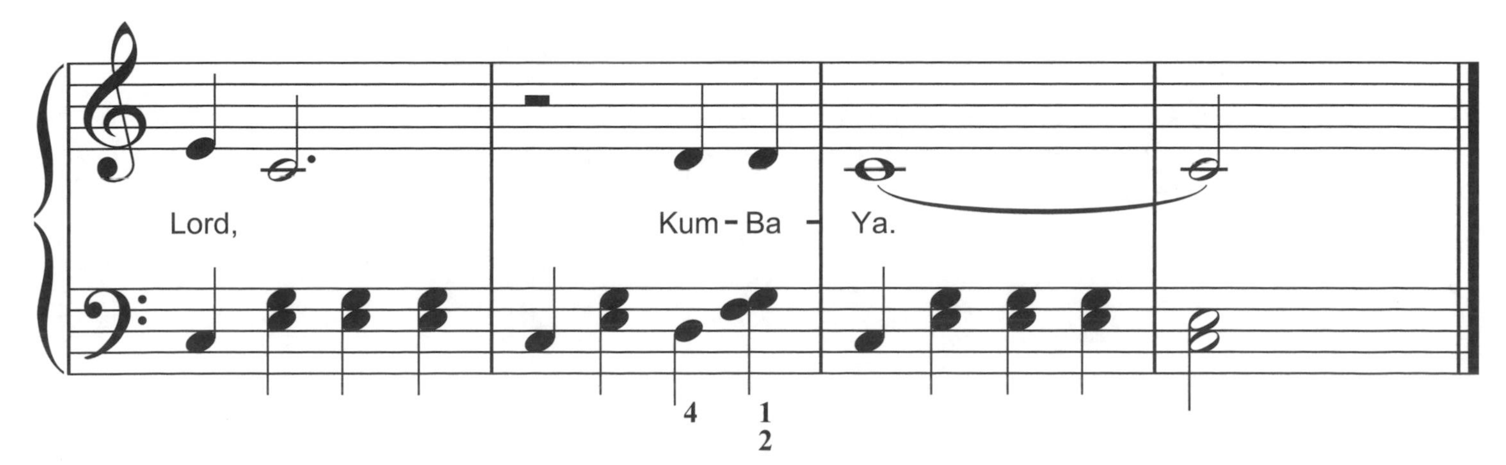

The Major Scale Formula

The major scale is the mother of all music. I call it this because most music starts from the major scale. There is a formula used to create a major scale using a series of whole steps and half steps. The pattern is: whole step, whole step, half step, whole step, whole step, whole step, half step, or commonly written:

W – W – H – W – W – W – H

If you start on any note and use this formula you will create a major scale. The starting note will also be the root note (or key). Here's an example: start with a root note middle C and play the C major scale.

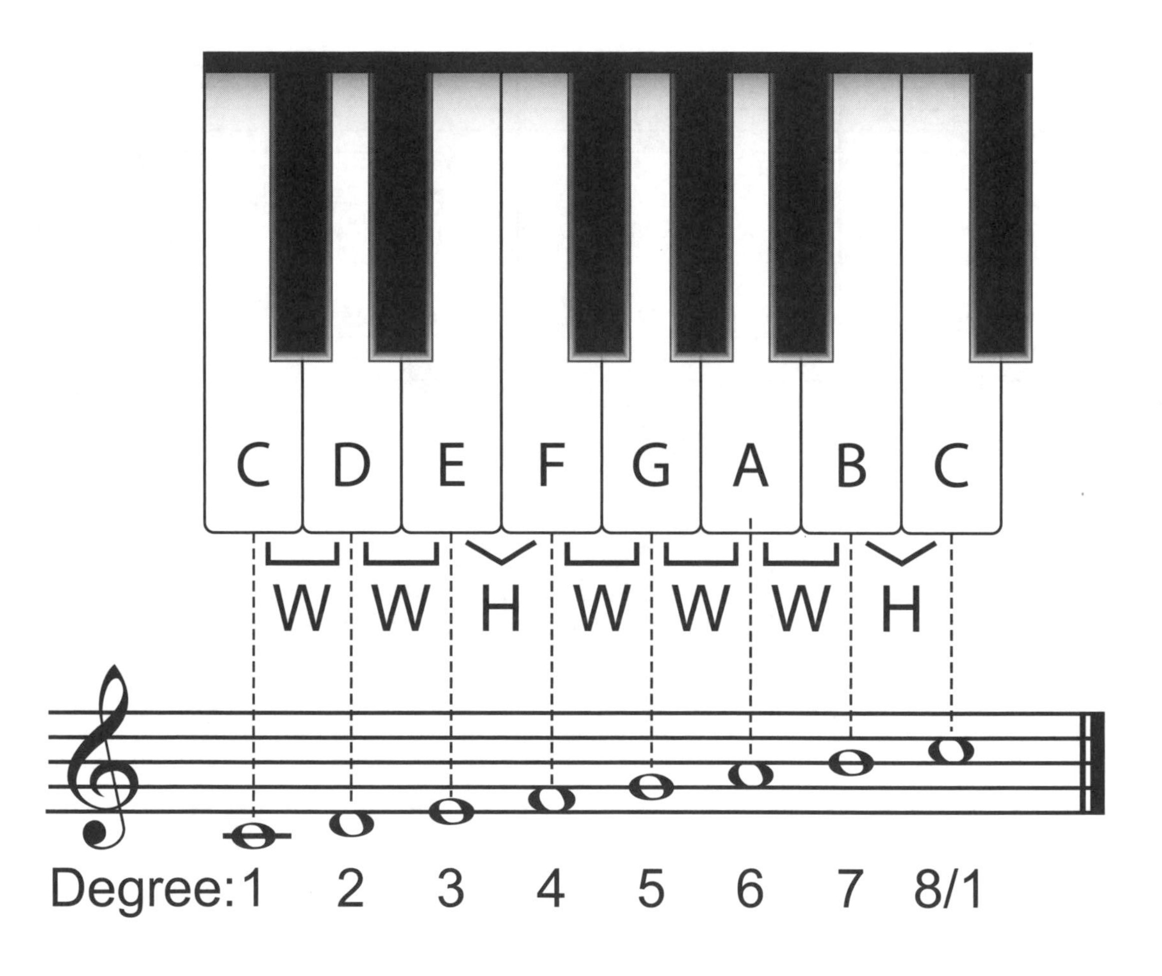

The C major scale is C – D – E – F – G – A – B – C. This will be the only natural scale, meaning the only major scale that won't need any sharps or flats to make the formula work. Every other scale will have at least one flat or one sharp.

Playing the C Major Scale

Because there are eight notes in the major scale to play this scale with one hand you will need to learn two finger crossings. For both of these crossings it is VERY important not to twist your wrist and to keep your fingers curved and palm open.

Ascending Cross Under

To play the C major scale ascending, start with your right hand thumb on the middle C and play C – D – E. Next cross your thumb under your middle finger to play the F note, and then continue with G – A – B – C. Follow the diagram below to play the C major scale ascending.

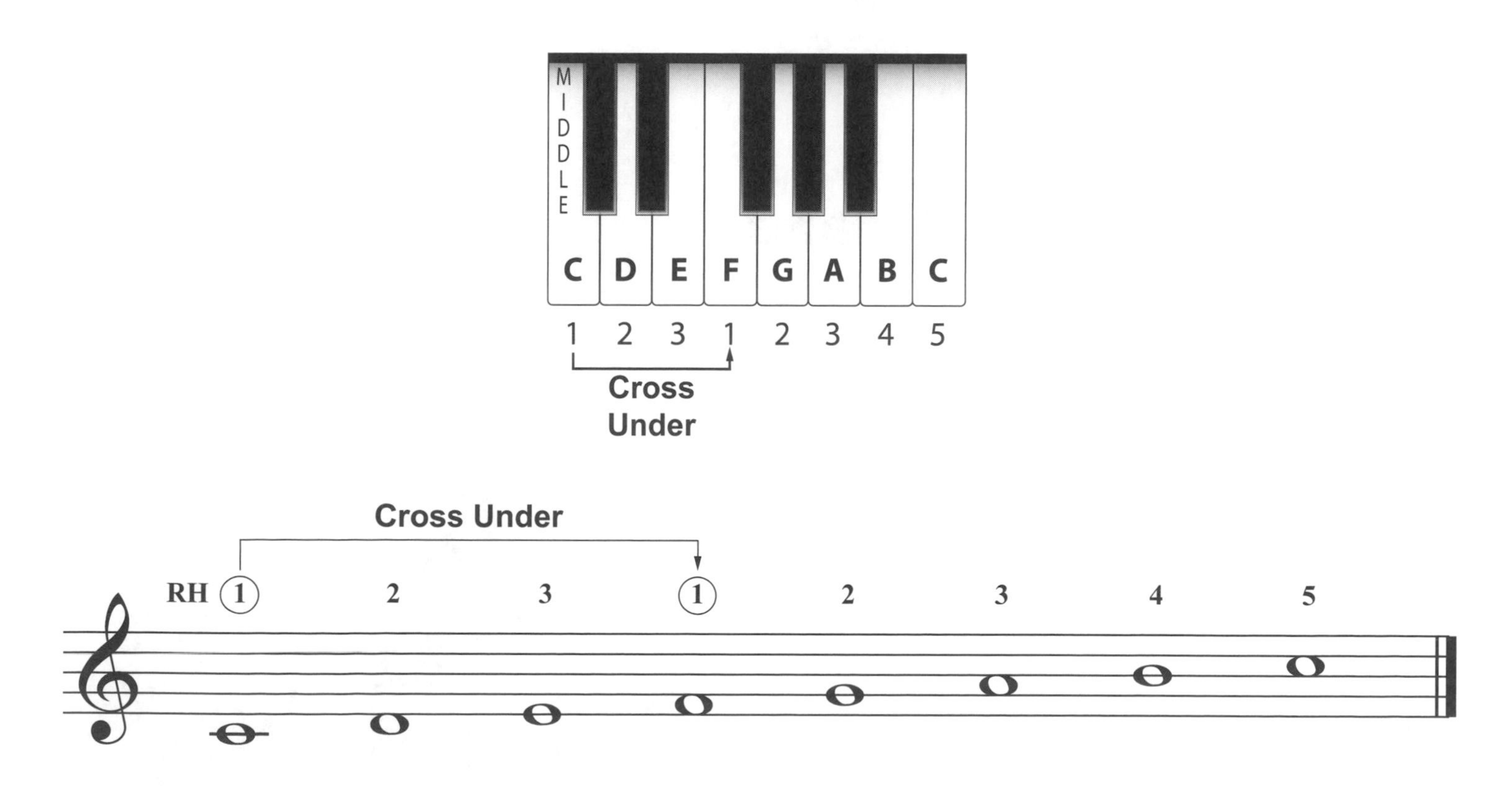

Descending Cross Over

Start at the last note of the scale with your pinky on the C note. Play down the scale C – B – A – G – F, then cross your middle finger over your thumb to the E note and finish the scale. Follow the diagram below to play the C major scale descending.

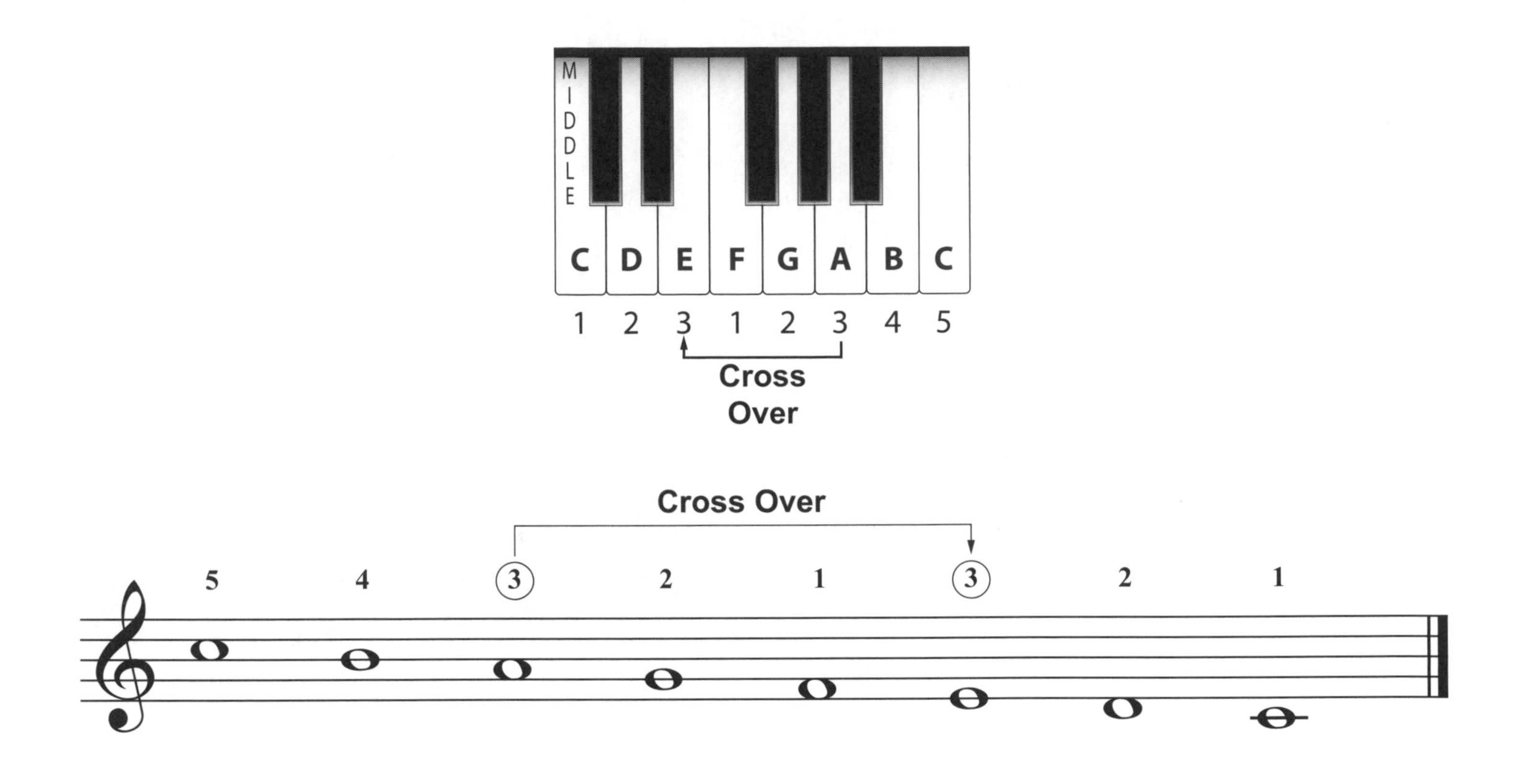

C Major Scale Left Hand

To play the C major scale with your left hand you will also have two finger crossings but they will be the opposite of the right hand. You will cross over ascending and under descending. To the right is a picture of the finger crossing with your left hand. Play the left hand C major scale on the next page.

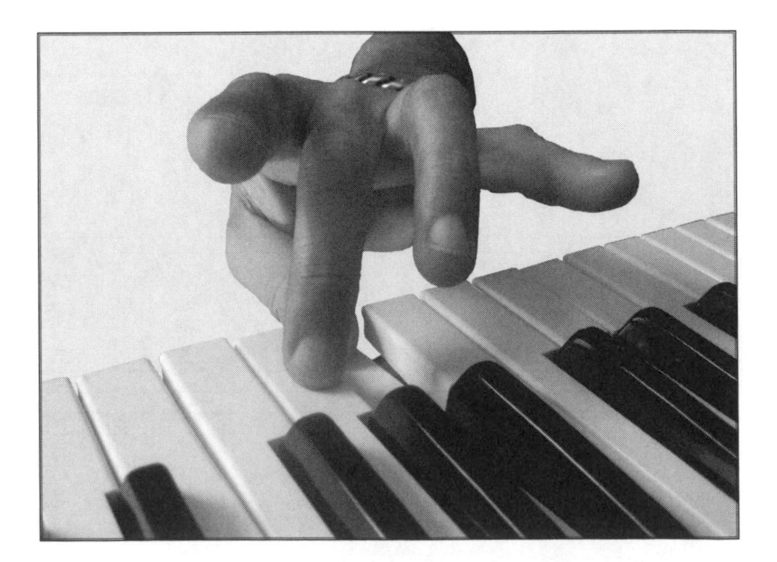

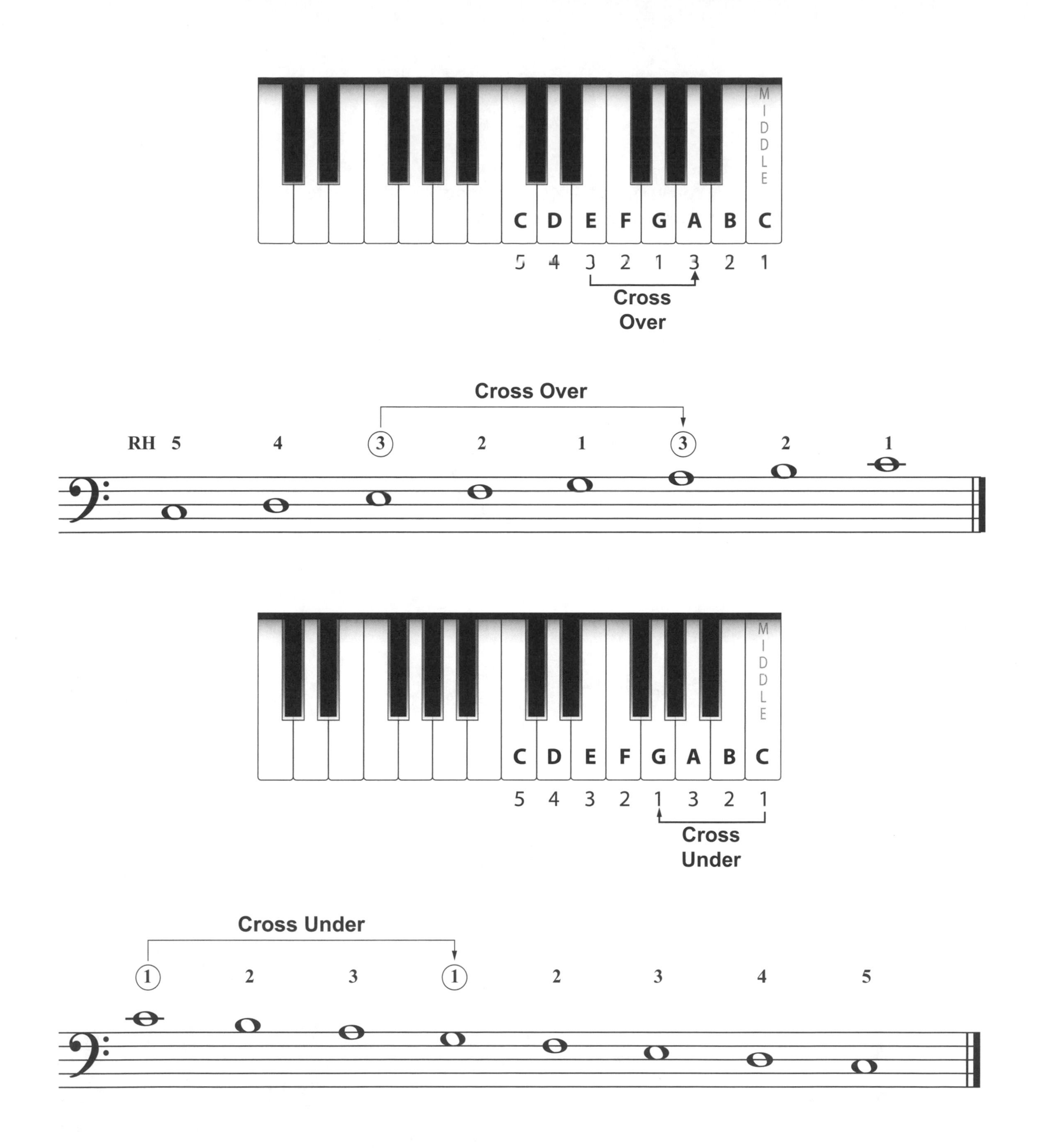

Learn Piano 2 - Quiz 2

Once you complete this section go to RockHouseSchool.com and take the quiz to track your progress. You will receive an email with your results and suggestions.

G Major Chord

Let's learn a new major chord. You will use the 4 – 3 method to find the notes to play the G major chord. Follow the diagram below and make sure to use the proper fingers:

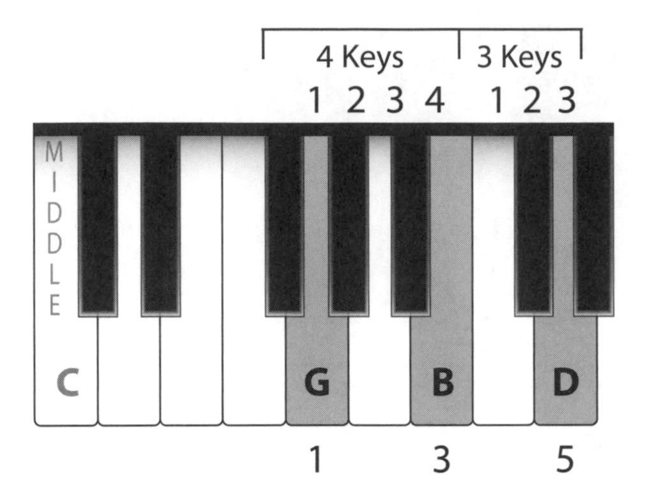

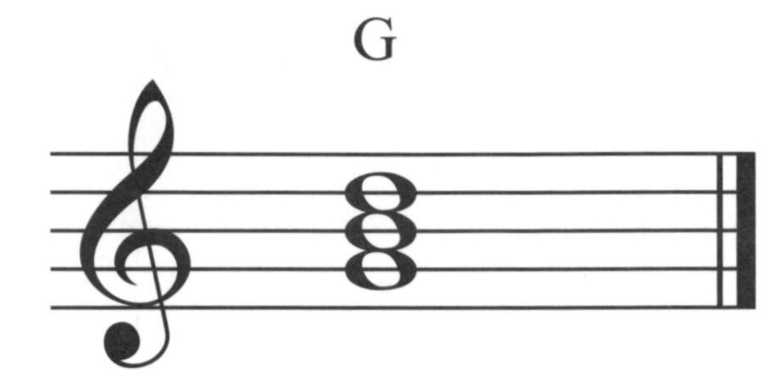

CD Track
68

The I – IV – V Chords

The I – IV – V chords are the most common chord combination in all music. Many hit songs have been written using this song structure. It is called a I – IV – V progression because you build chords from the 1st, 4th and 5th notes in the major scale. A I – IV – V progression in the key of "C" would be C – F and G major chords. Below are the diagrams for all three chords. Play them one after another and hear the sound of this chord progression.

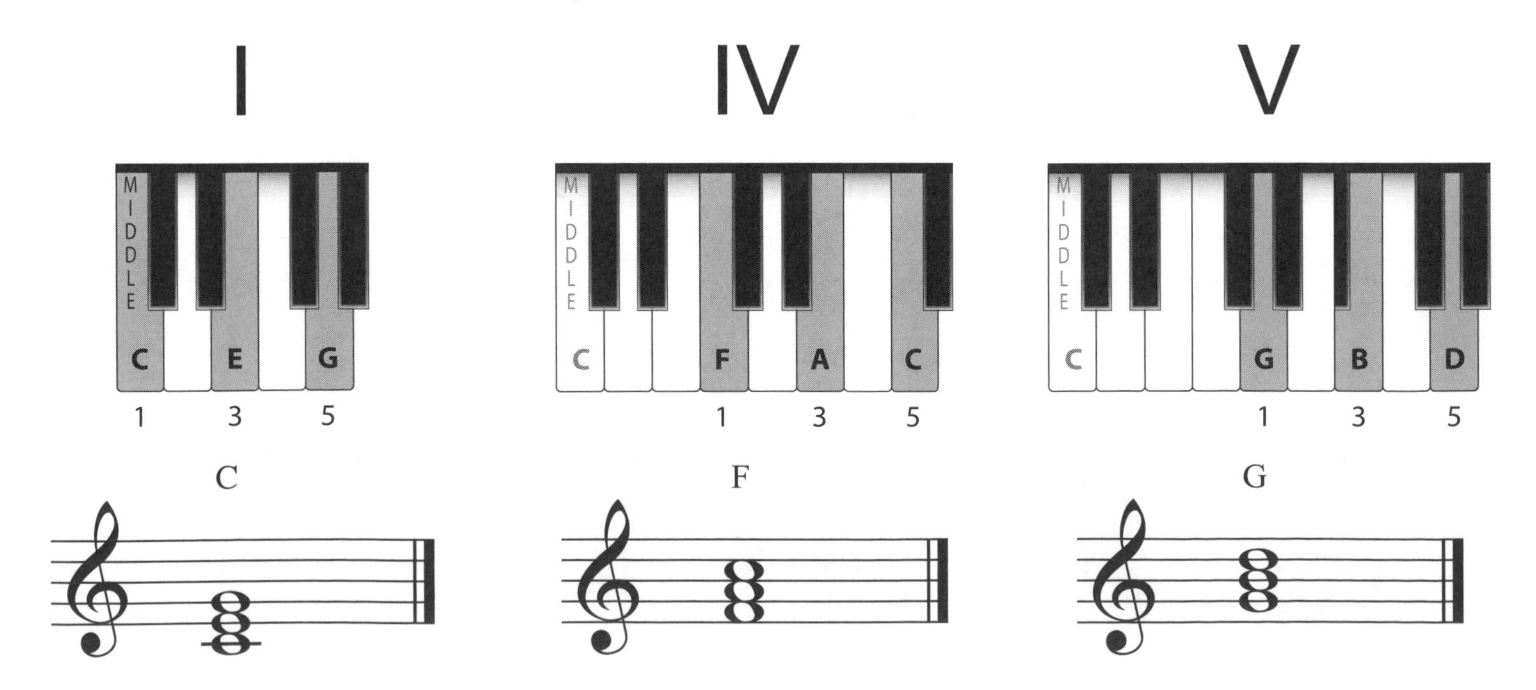

Adding Bass Notes

Now add a lower note to each chord as a bass note. This gives the chord a full sound almost like adding a bass guitar. Play each of the I – IV – V chords with the bass notes.

C Major

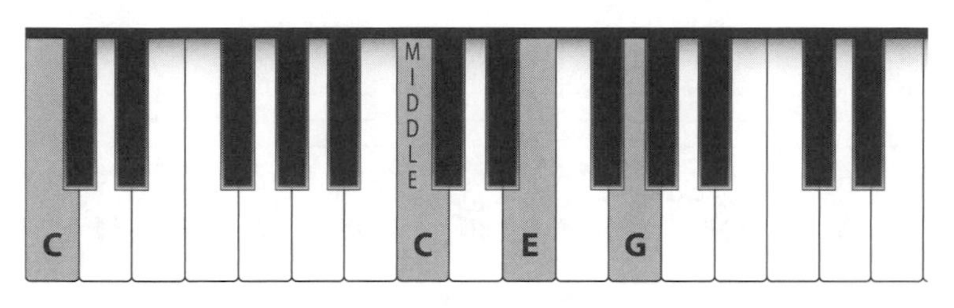

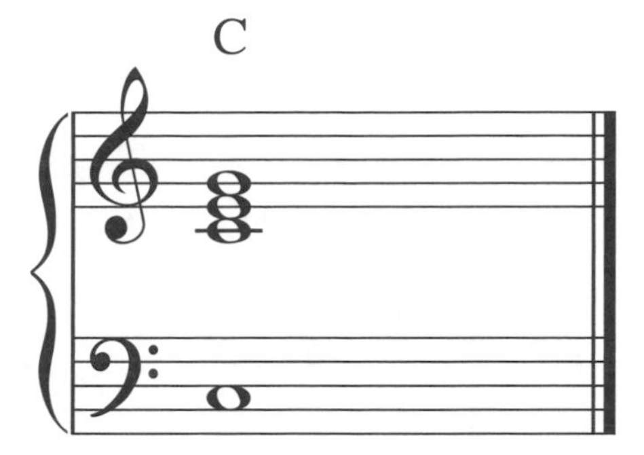

F Major

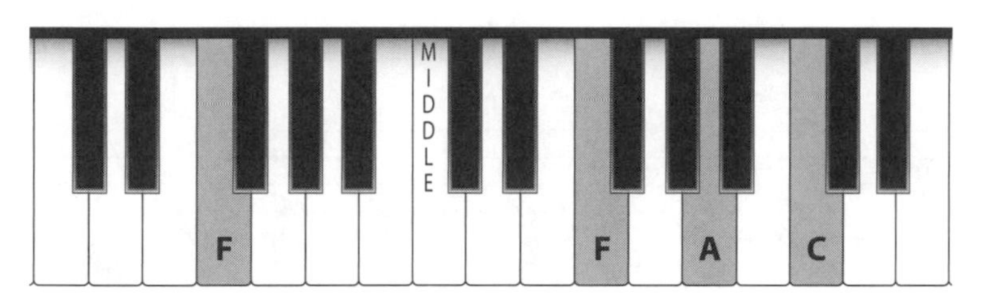

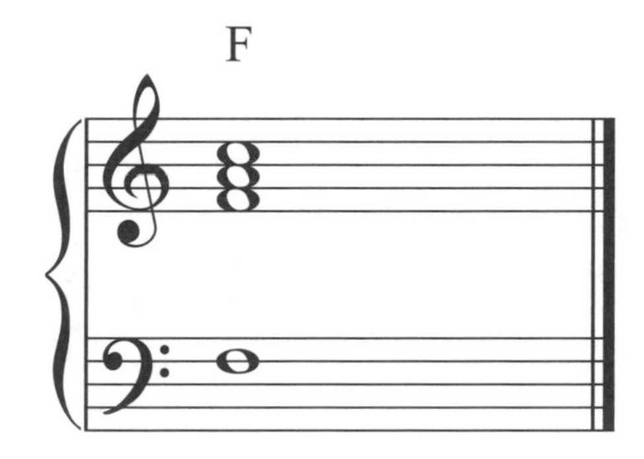

G Major

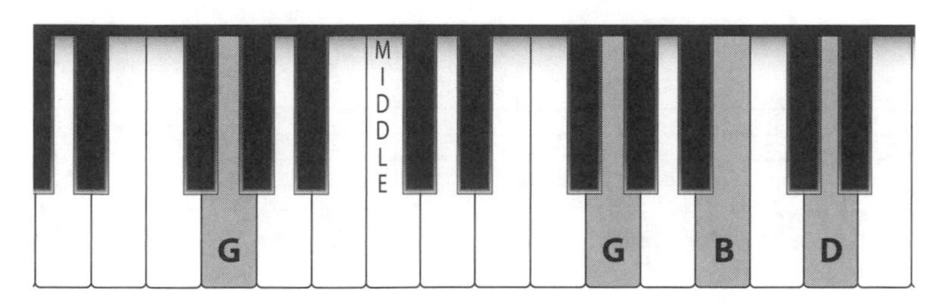

The I – IV – V 12 Bar Blues

The I – IV – V progression is often used in a 12 bar blues structure. This means that there are 12 measures that form the progression before repeating. Below is a 12 bar blues progression:

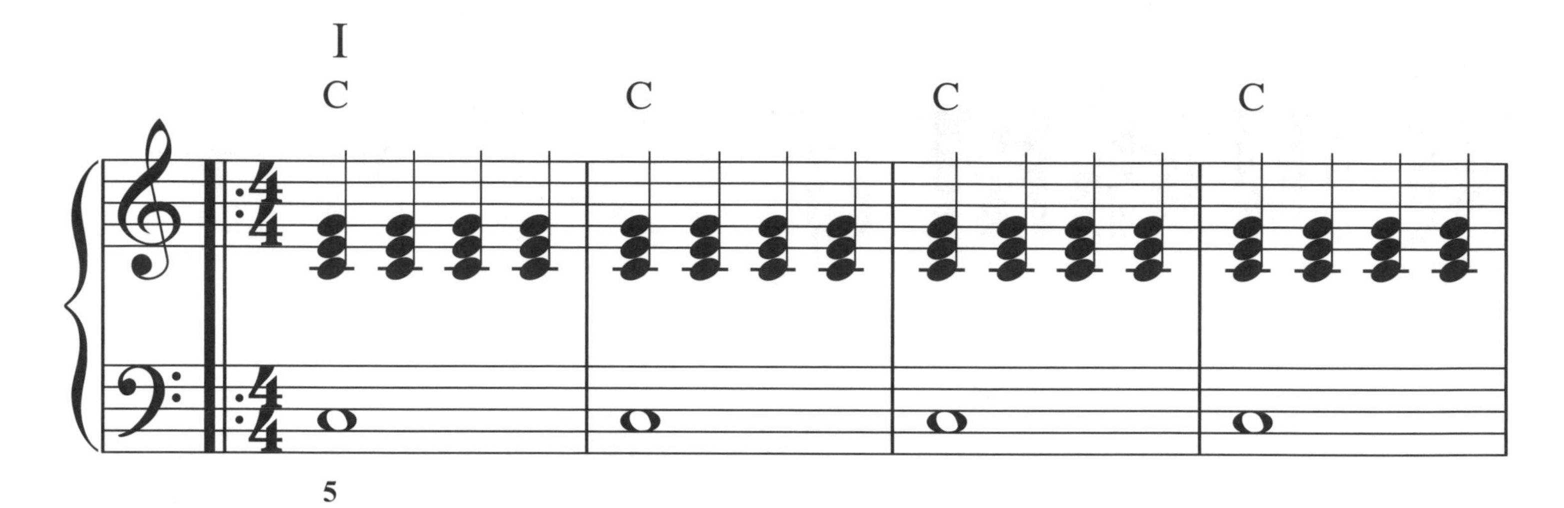

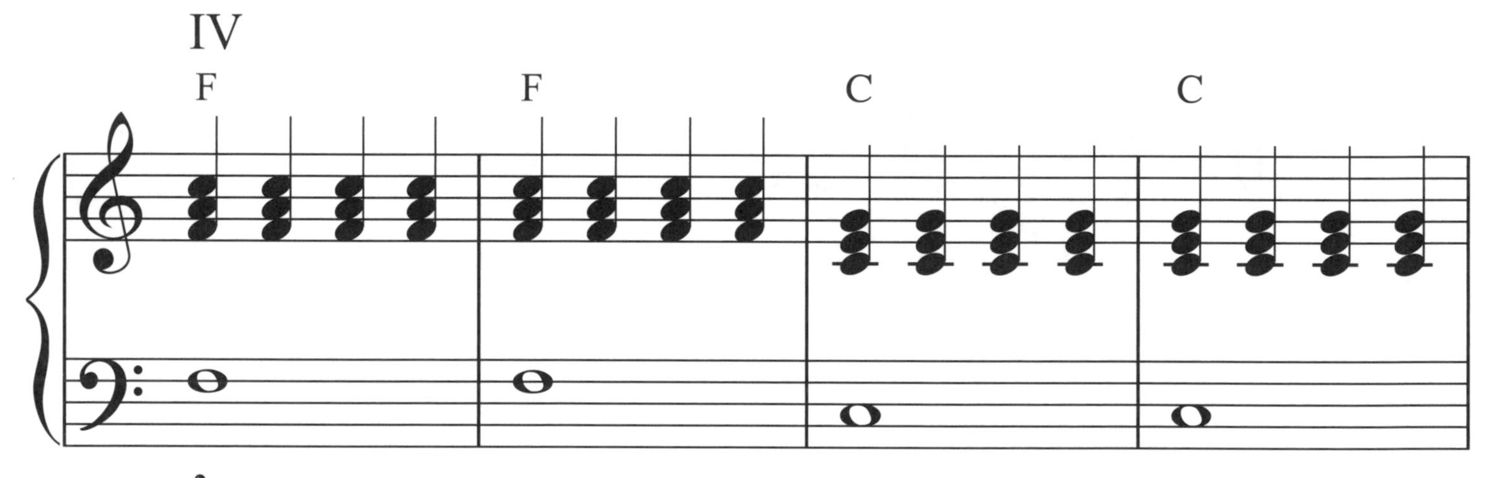

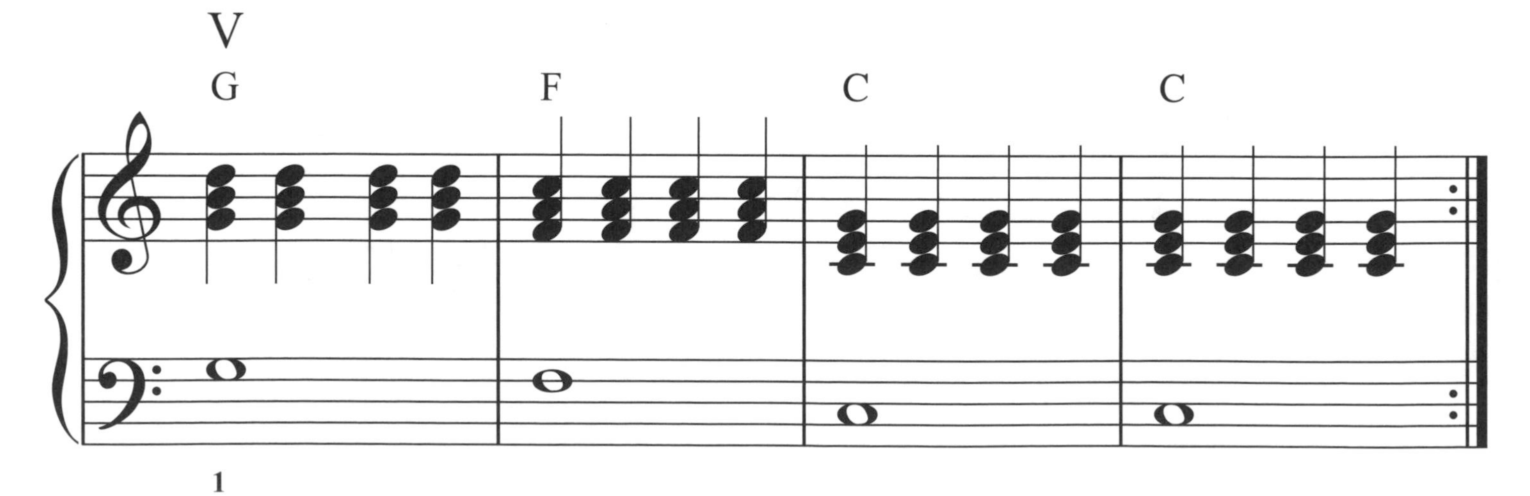

Chord Inversions

An inversion, by definition, is to turn something upside down. For chord inversions you take the notes and rearrange them in a different order. One reason this is done is to keep your hand in a small area on the keyboard and still be able to play many chords. We will be constructing 1st inversions for the C, F and G major chords. To play a 1st inversion take the bottom note (root note) and move it to the top of the chord. For the C major chord take the C note and move it to the top and the chord notes will be E – G – C. See the diagram below and play this inversion:

C Major

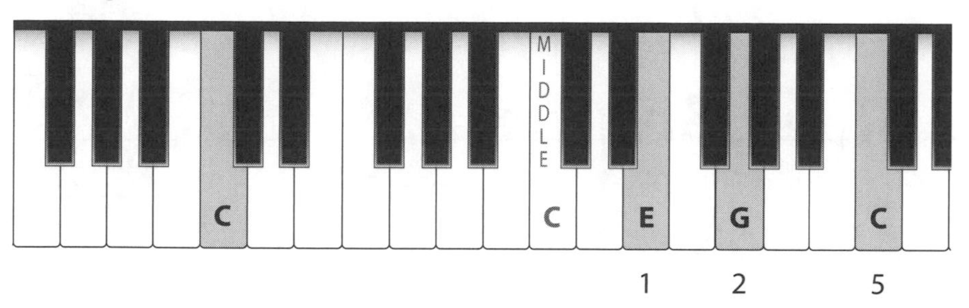

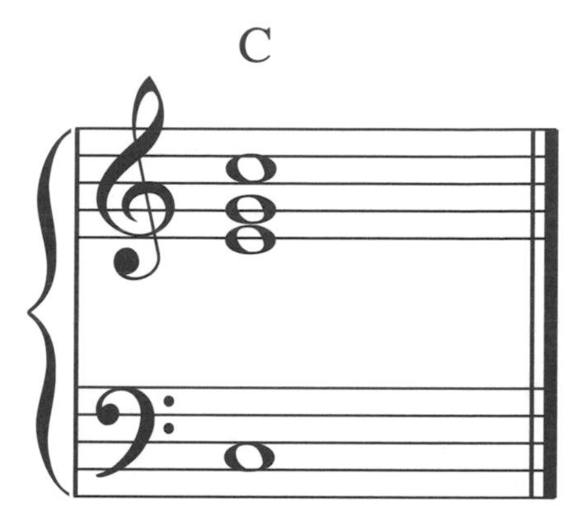

Next, play the 1st inversion F and G major chords in the same fashion. For F major, take the F note and move it to the top so the order would be A – C – F. For G major take the G root note and move it to the top of the chord so the notes in order will be B – D – G. I have presented these two chords an octave lower then you played them previously because you will use them this way in the next lesson. After you play the chord with the right hand add the left hand bass note.

F Major

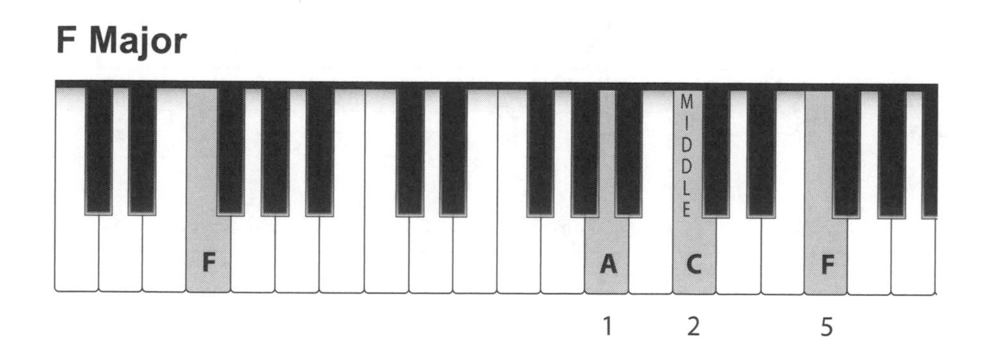

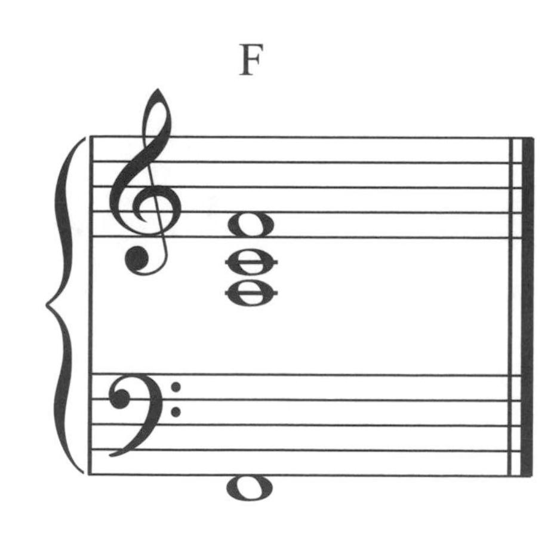

G Major

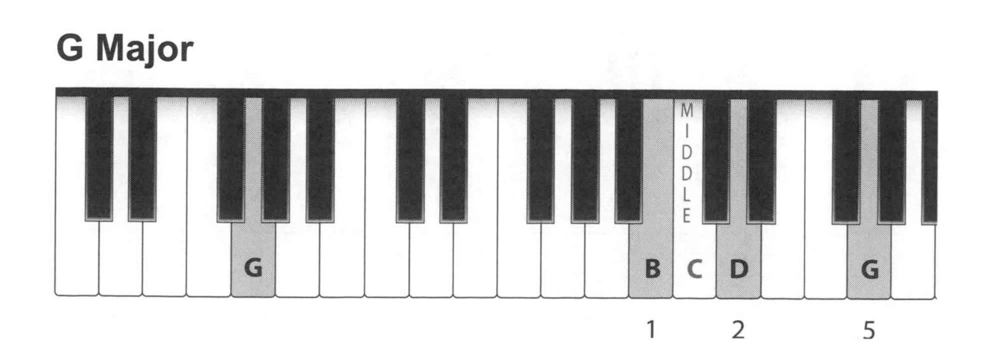

The Blues Feel

The 12 bar blues you learned had a steady quarter note feel. The blues often has uneven or syncopated rhythms. One common blues feel combines eighth, dotted quarter and quarter notes to create a syncopated rhythm. Play the following rhythm example to understand the feel. The last chord is played with staccato and should be cut short.

The Blues Shuffle

Next, you will apply this blues feel to the 12 bar blues using the chord inversions for the F and G chords; make sure to play over the backing track to apply this lesson in a band fashion. The last measure contains eighth notes that should be played with a blues swing feel to them and not played as even eighth notes.

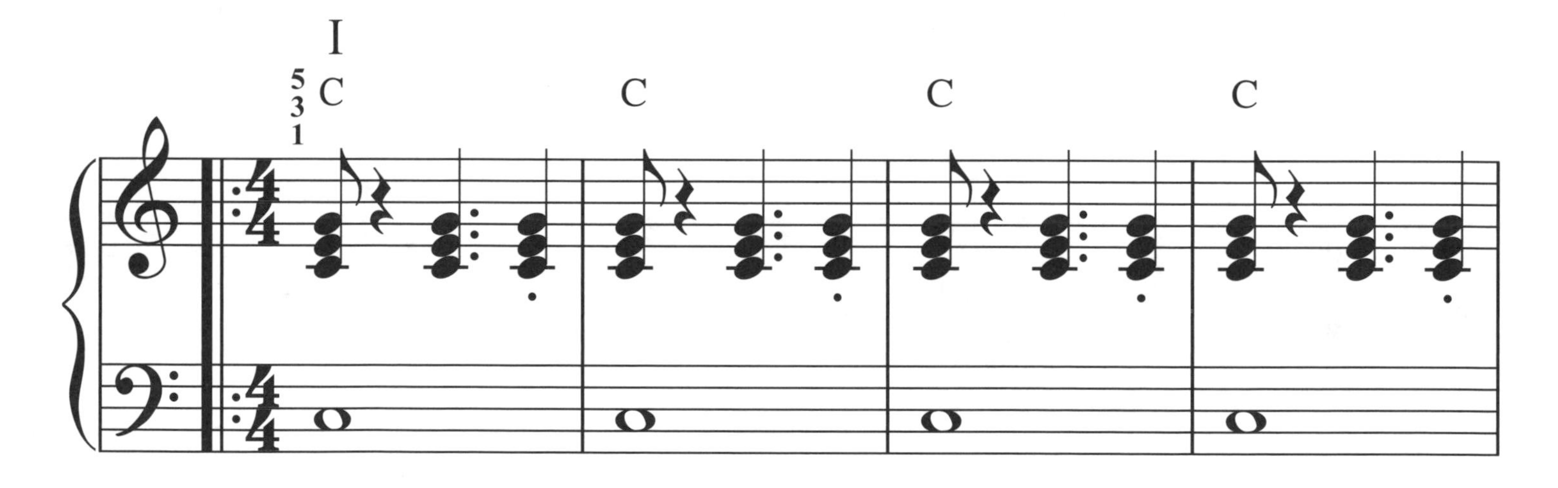

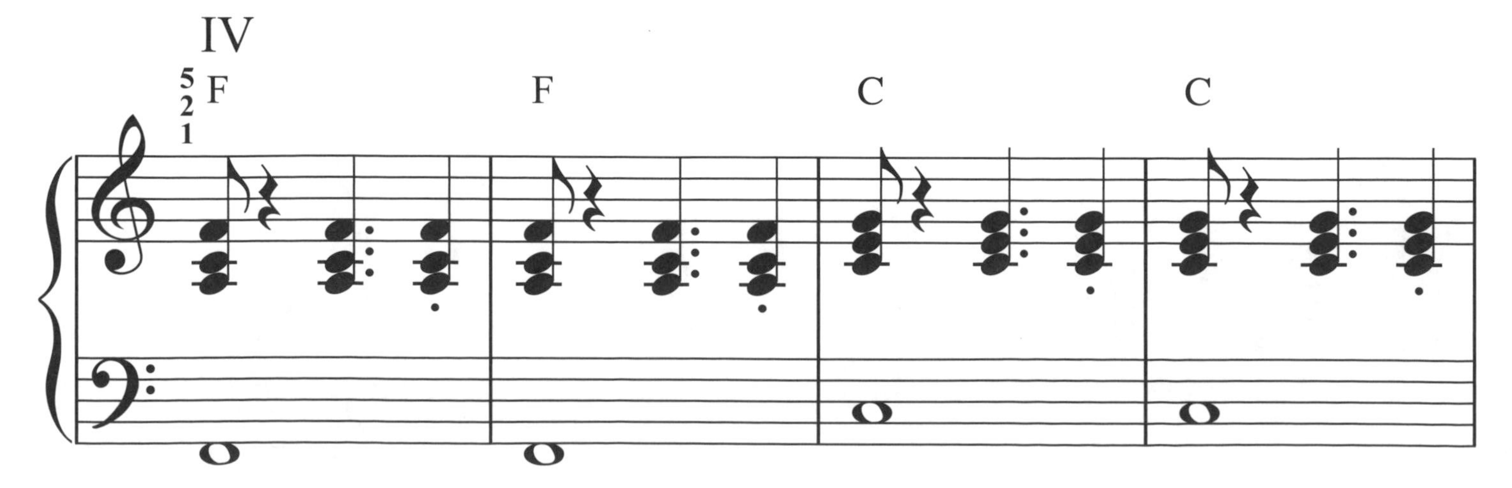

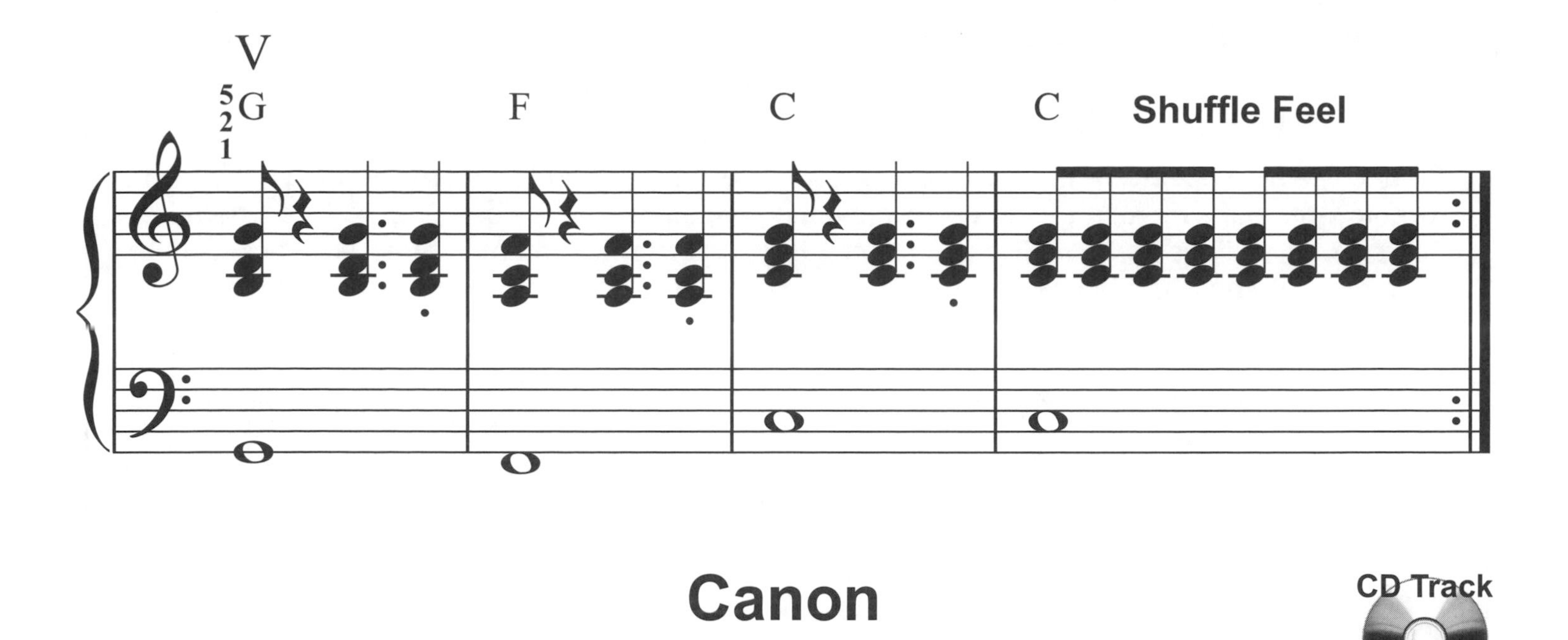

Canon

CD Track
80-82

Canon is a very popular classical progression. I have outlined the chord progression above the staff so you can see and hear where each chord is played. You will be playing intervals that you learned earlier in the book with your right hand, take note of these. The intervals played with G and F are inverted 5ths. This means that the root is on top and the interval becomes a 4th stacked this way. We will get deeper into theory of intervals in Book 3.

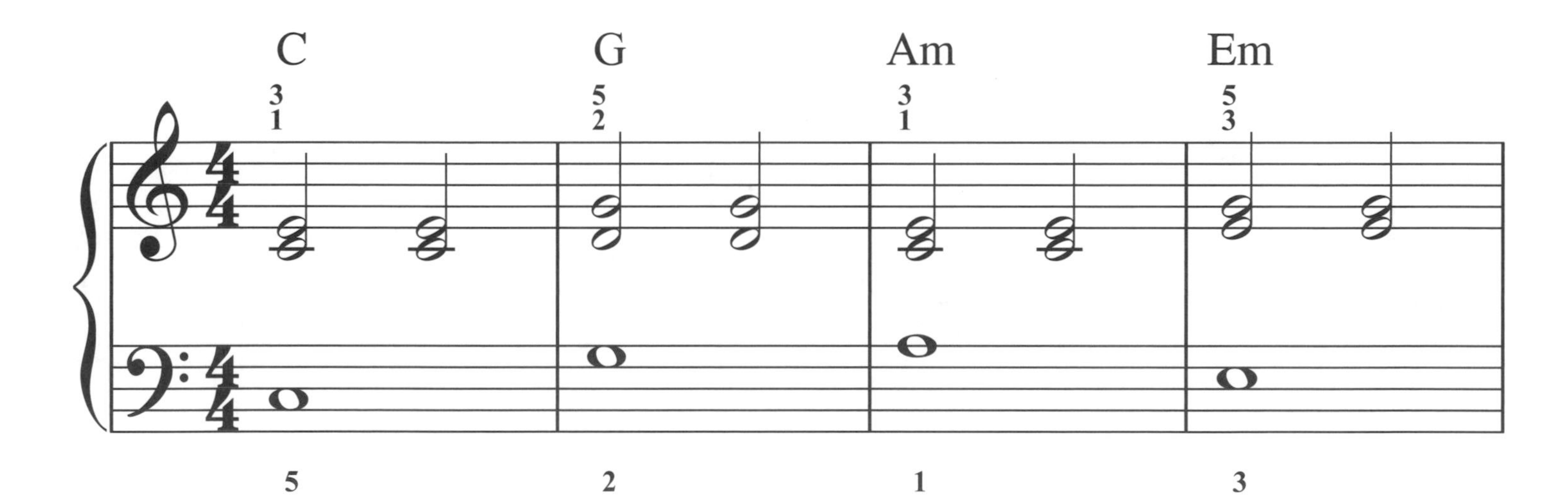

F C F G G7

4 1 3 1 4 1 5 2 4 2

2 5 2 1

First & Second Endings

Sometimes a composer wants to repeat a section in a song and add a different ending but doesn't want to write out everything all over again creating pages and pages of music. This is where first and second endings come in. First and second endings are notated by numbered brackets over each ending. The endings can be any number of measures in length. In the example below each ending is one measure in length. Note the repeat sign between the endings. This means that you play through ending one, go back to the beginning play up to the first ending, skip the first ending and play the second ending. Play through the example below. In the next lesson you will use first and second endings within a song.

Dreaming Messiah

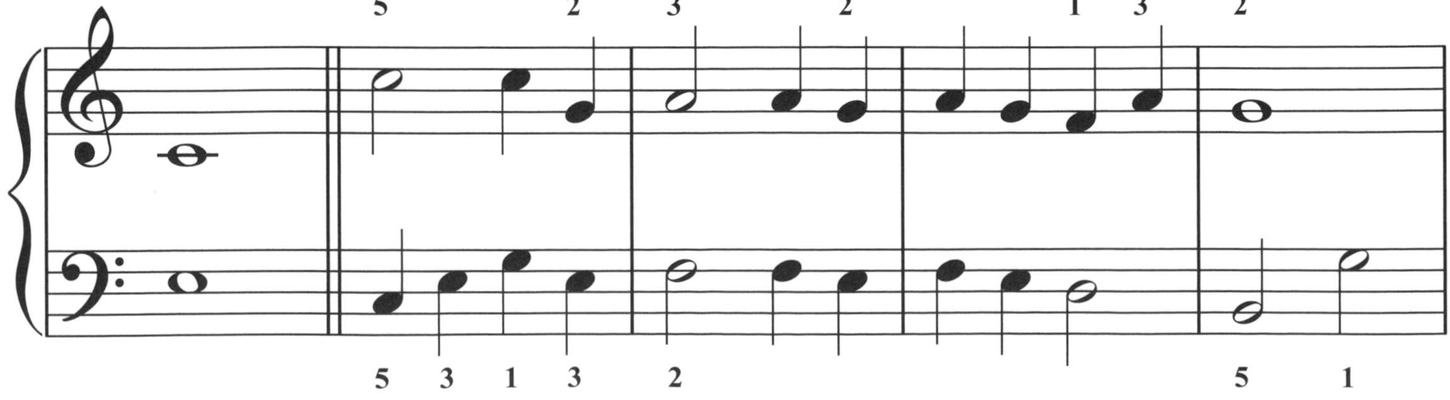

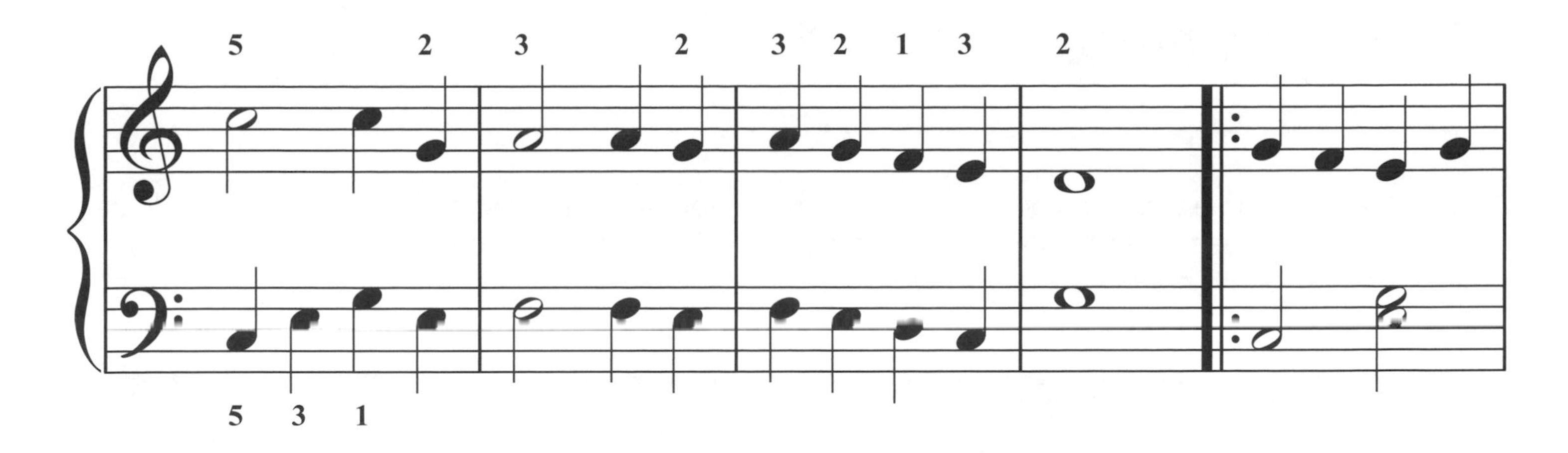

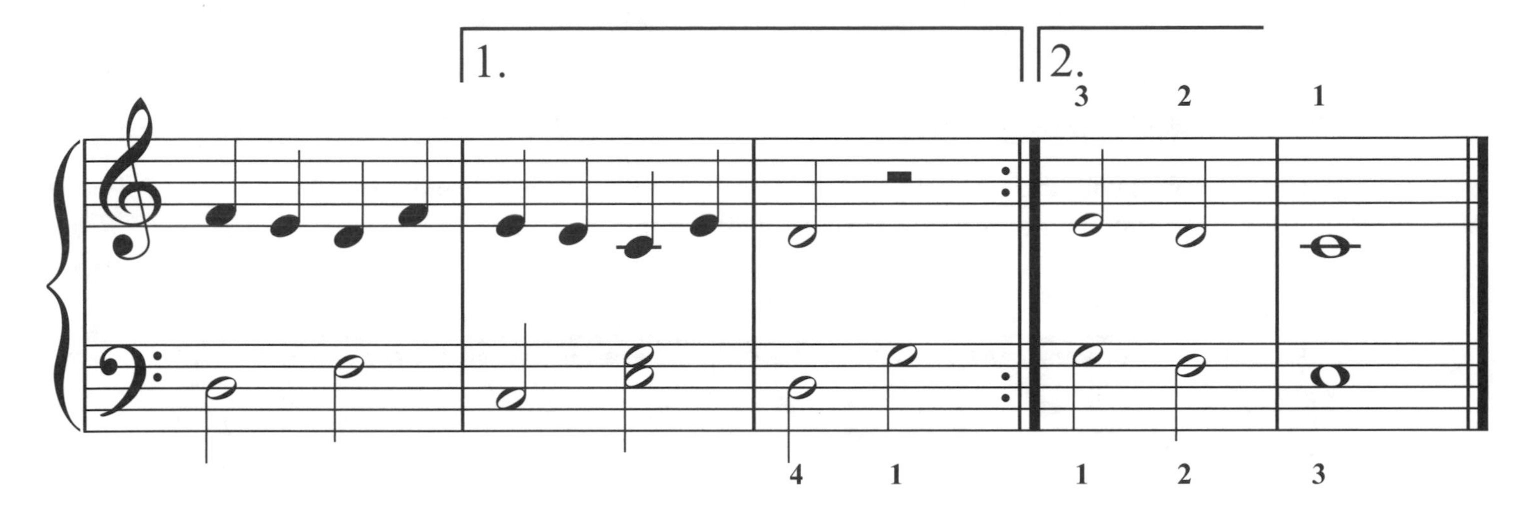

Primary Chords

Chords derived from the root, 4th and 5th degrees of a major scale are called primary chords. You have already learned to play the I – IV – V chords in the key of "C" major, now you will learn where they come from. On the staff below, if you only played the bottom note of each chord you would play a C major scale. Notice all of the chords, as well as the primary chords, are derived from the C major scale.

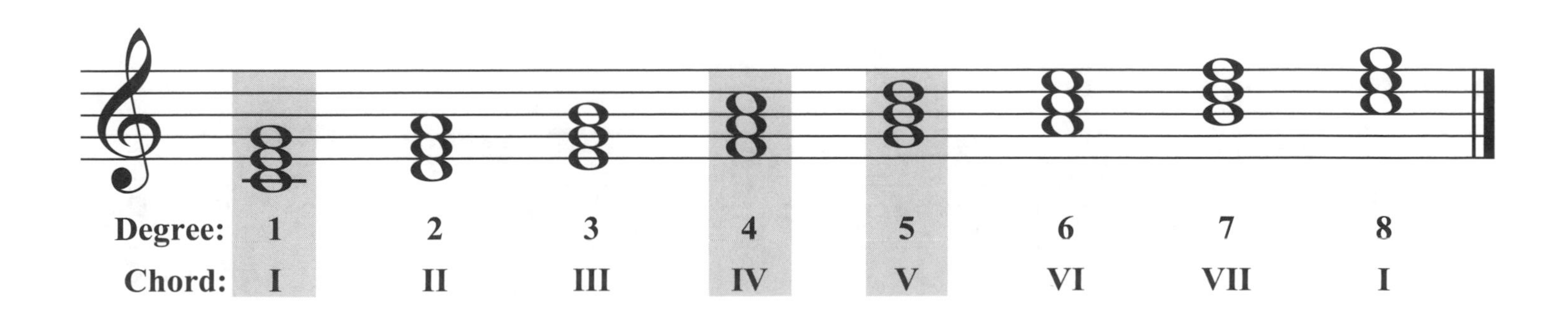

Sixteenth Notes

To play the following exercises you will need to know sixteenth notes. A sixteenth note receives ¼ beat of sound. It subdivides one beat into four equal sections. Sixteenth notes are twice as fast as an eighth note. Count sixteenth notes now as follows:

Now play sixteenth notes with the C major chord to understand and feel the timing. Accent the first note of each four note sequence to accentuate the feel of this timing.

Single Note Exercises #2

Here are more exercises to help challenge your hands to build coordination. Make sure to keep the notes in a steady tempo and build up speed gradually. I recommend using a metronome to help gauge your progress. Write down your metronome tempos and see how much speed you can develop in a few weeks time. These exercises should be practiced daily. Even experienced players still practice these to warm their fingers up before playing.

Example 1 - Right Hand

Example 2 - Right Hand

Example 3 - Left Hand

Example 4 - Left Hand

Example 5 - Both Hands

Example 6 - Both Hands

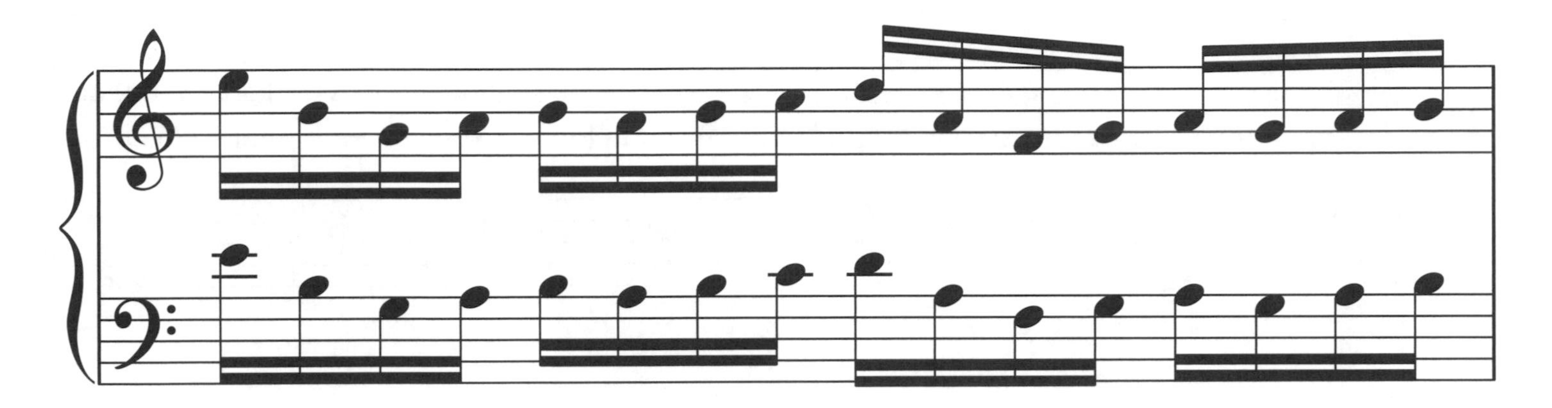

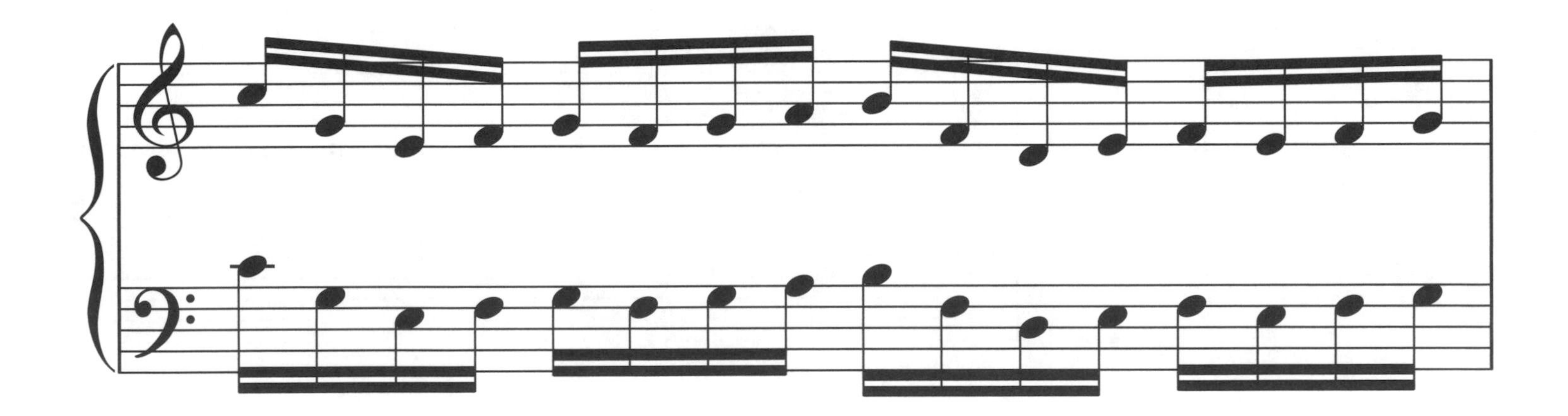

The Star Spangled Banner

This song introduces a lower A note being played with your right hand. Look at the keyboard diagram to see the notes location.

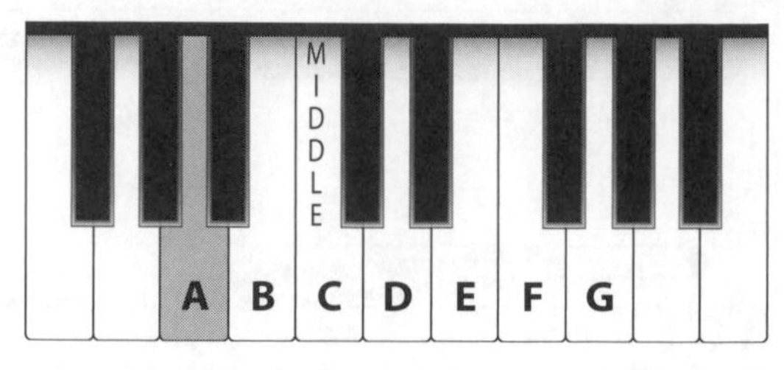

Andante

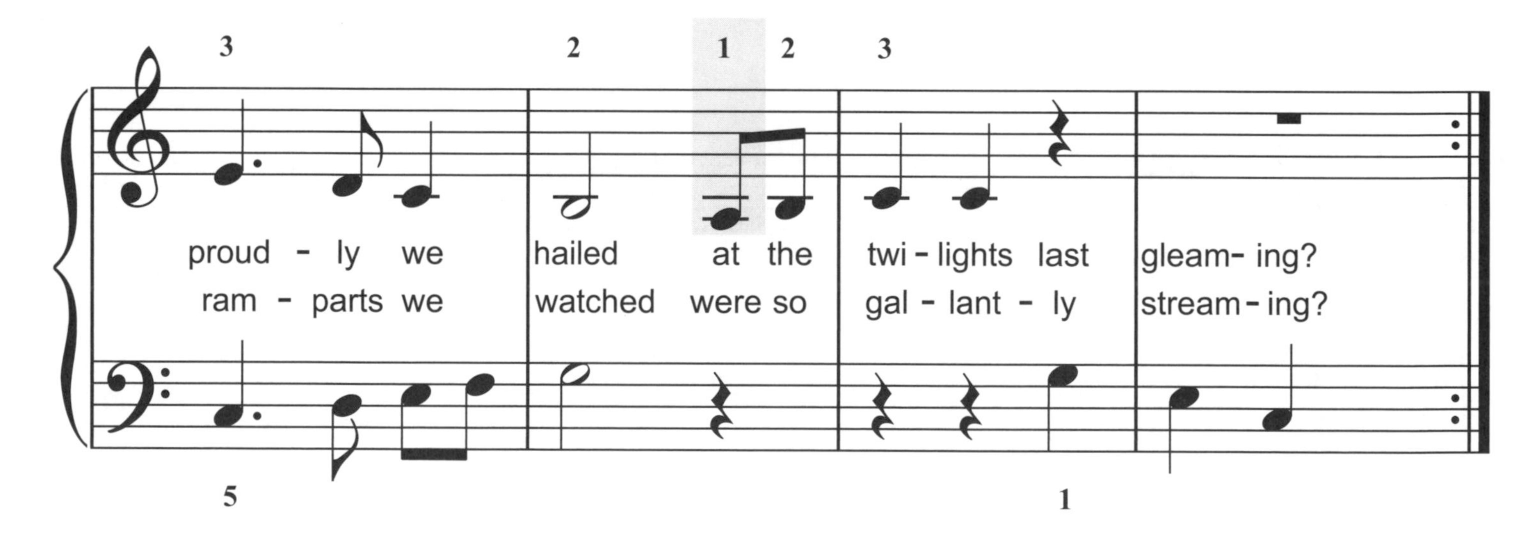

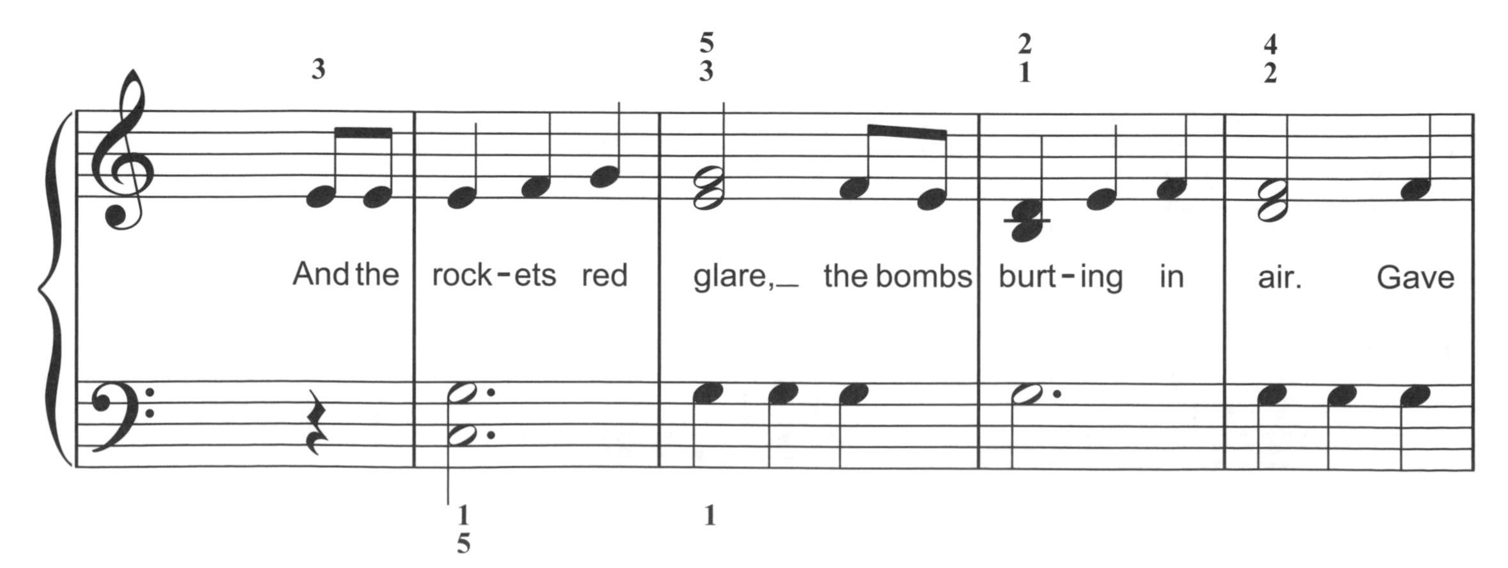

Fermata

= Fermata

A fermata indicates that a note is sustained longer than its written note value. The exact time of how long its held is at the discretion of the performer; however, a sustained note that is double the time value is not unusual. I have outlined in the previous song where you will find the fermata.

Spring

From ***The Four Seasons***

A. Vivaldi

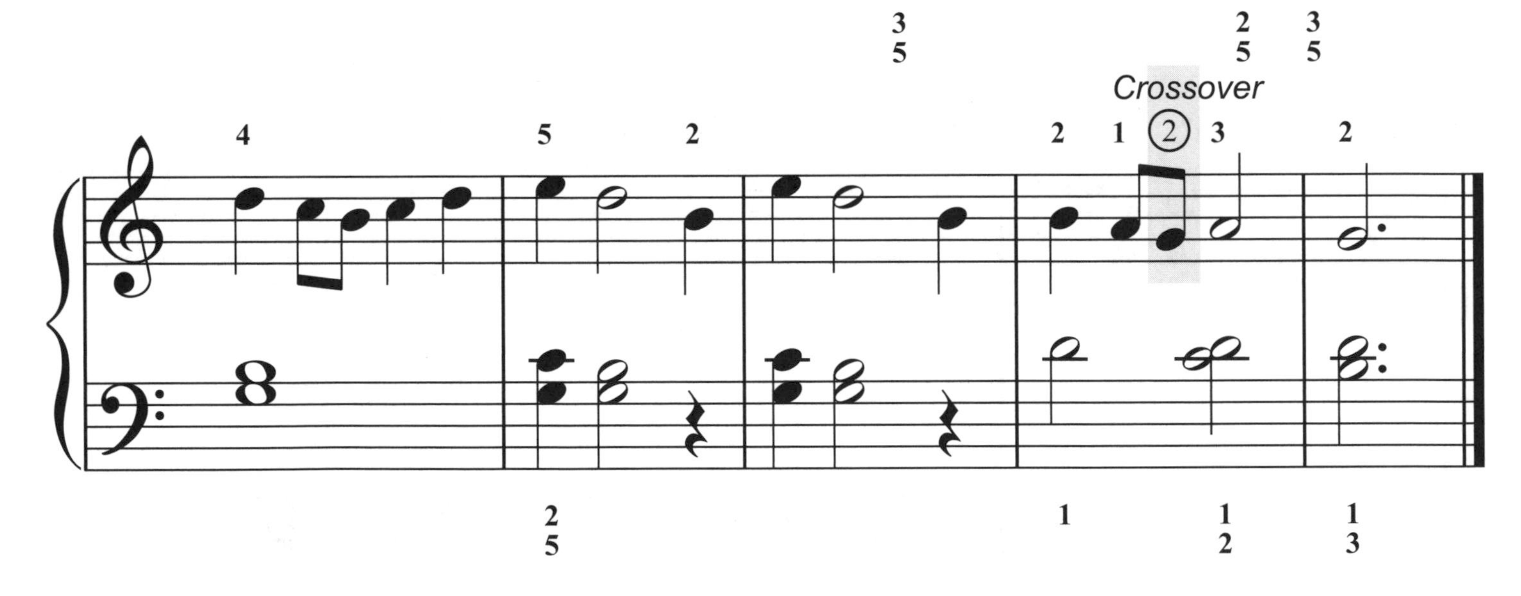

Learn Piano 2 - Quiz 3

Congratulations you've made it to the end of Book 2! Go to RockHouseSchool.com and take the quiz to track your progress. You will receive an email with your results and an official Rock House Method "Certificate of Completion" when you pass.

Appendix

Musical Words

Accent – To play harder or louder.

Arpeggio – The notes of a chord played separately.

Beat – The regular pulse of music which may be dictated by a metronome, or by the accents in music.

Chord – The sounding of three or more notes simultaneously.

Dominant 7th Chord – A chord constructed with the 1st – 3rd – 5th – and b7 degrees of a major scale. Also known as a 7th chord.

Dynamics – The variation of sound levels, louder and softer.

Flat – An accidental symbol placed to the left of a note, indicating that its pitch should be lowered by a half step.

Gig – When a band or musician plays a show.

Interval – The distance between two pitches.

Measure – A musical term signifying the smallest division of a song, containing a fixed number of beats, marked off by vertical lines on the staff. The distance between two bar lines on a musical staff.

Melody – A succession of single tones containing rhythm and pitches arranged as a musical shape.

Octave – An interval spanning seven diatonic degrees (eleven half-steps). An octave above C would be C.

Progression – A series of chords that are played within a song.

Root Note – The tonic or fundamental note of a chord. The note which gives a chord or scale its letter name.

Scale – A series of notes in ascending or descending order that presents the pitches of a key or mode, beginning and ending on the tonic of that key or mode.

Syncopation – Deliberate altering of the meter or pulse of a composition by a temporarily shifting the accent to a weak beat or an off-beat.

Turnaround – A short phrase at the end of a progression that brings the player back to the beginning of the song in a smooth transition.

Word Search

Go to RockHouseSchool.com to get the solution to the following puzzles.

```
O L I I D J U O T U U Y S Y D N S C K M T E L O T
E I G H T H N O T E S T K Y P E R I C A H L A P K
S N G N X O C P P R A Z N Q T E S D V J E A D M F
S I O L H F D F N C G A X O O U H O T O G C E N N
V H G I P S D N C A M U N A M Z P T U R R S P T H
S Q A G S E Z A E I D H Q T W V A T U S A R R A P
F L Y R R S T O C C T Y H D I K F E D C N O E A J
I Y A M P O E M S H S C R D M F W D R A D J P S F
B X Q V O S A R G N A E X T I M W Q X L S A M B B
Z D Y X R R A I G N J Q R V L J V U Q E T M A X E
Y C K J K E E N E O Q M D C C A T A A F A E D I V
E Q H I V D T N D R R C J N X N Z R G O F H I P W
G P N K E T E N B F G P L W J O Z T E R F T Y Q R
N G S T X I J G I J L R D E W Y B E T M A X D A Z
S E T I L V W T Y C S A I R G G E R G U M Q C U I
I O V K N I A T S U S L T J O L Y N U L G G N J P
D U N E Z P T P X L O K W S I H Q O E A X Q A O L
E I S E T O N H T N E E T X I S C T E Z X Z C E L
E P R I M A R Y C H O R D S E R N E R Z C A C G X
Y L B Z O C M P T E U H A L C H O S T T X H C I R
Q B Q N H C B X A Y Y H B M Q N U H F U U U H E K
D F V O H E F W N W D E O Y U V R M P I R G E J S
W I R W K M O B I O J B N W B K M Z T G I U U H B
E D A M R O J A M C H L S M E E O X K H X E V M G
S I V O E L J Q A S D U O R W T D Q C E U G X W W
```

Search Words:

- Chord Progression
- Chords
- C Major
- Crescendo
- Damper Pedal
- Dotted Eighth Notes
- Dotted Quarter Notes
- Sixteenth Notes
- Staccato
- Sustain
- Tempo
- The Grand Staff
- The Major Scale

Crossword Puzzle

Across:

1. The tonic or fundamental note of a chord. The note which gives a chord or scale its letter name.
3. Gradually softer.
5. Ode to ______.
6. Fast.
7. A curved line that connects a group of notes indicates that you play them smoothly together in a flowing motion.
9. ______ Lang Syne.
10. A series of notes in ascending or descending order that presents the pitches of a key or mode, beginning and ending on the tonic of that key or mode.
11. A small dot placed on top or bottom of a note that indicates that you cut the note short and detached not letting it ring out.
13. A series of chords that are played within a song.
16. A small arrow placed on top or bottom of a note that indicates that you play the note louder.
18. A musical term signifying the smallest division of a song, containing a fixed number of beats, marked off by vertical lines on the staff. The distance between two bar lines on a musical staff.
21. A succession of single tones containing rhythm and pitches arranged as a musical shape.
22. Type of note that subdivides one beat into four equal sections.
23. The variation of sound levels, louder and softer.

Down:

2. Moderato.
4. Gradually louder.
6. The notes of a chord played separately.
8. A short phrase at the end of a progression that brings the player back to the beginning of the song in a smooth transition.
9. Slow.
10. Deliberate altering of the meter or pulse of a composition by a temporarily shifting the accent to a weak beat or an off-beat.
12. The combination of the treble and bass staffs together.
14. A variable speed device used to keep even time when playing.
15. An eighth note has a solid head, stem and a ________.
17. Chords derived from the Root, 4th and 5th degrees.
19. The smallest interval in music.
20. When you rearrange the notes of a chord into a different order.

Chord Glossary

Amaj^7

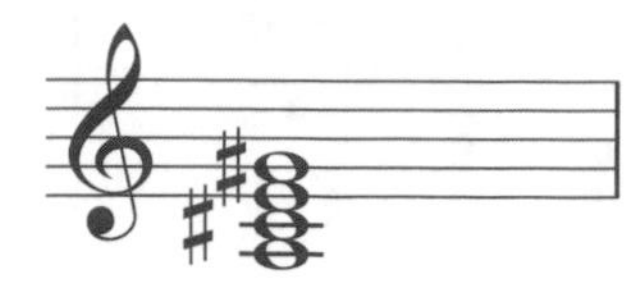

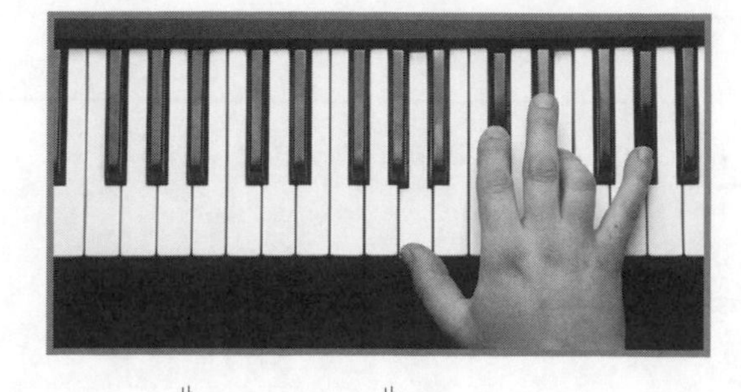

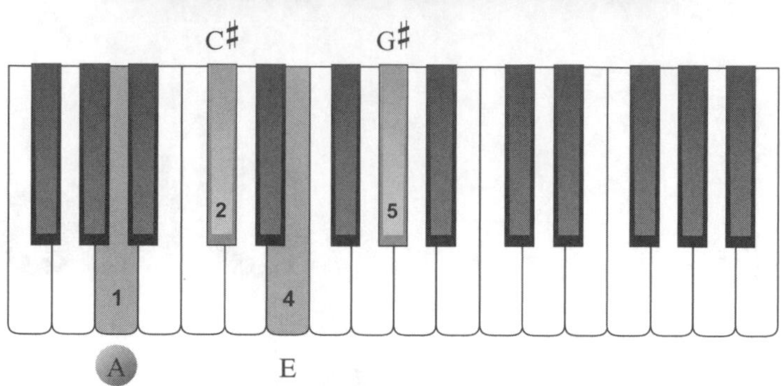

A^7

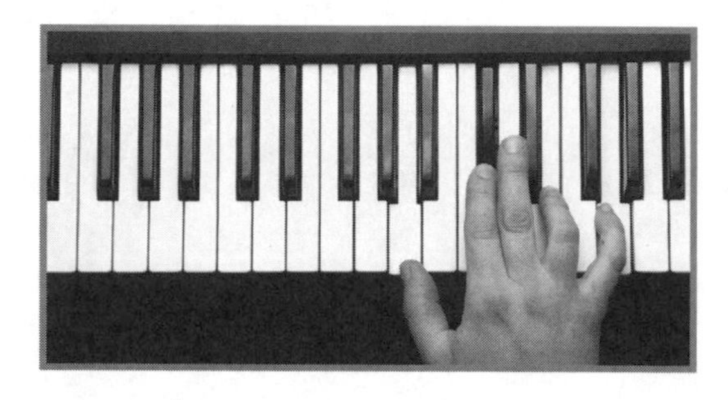

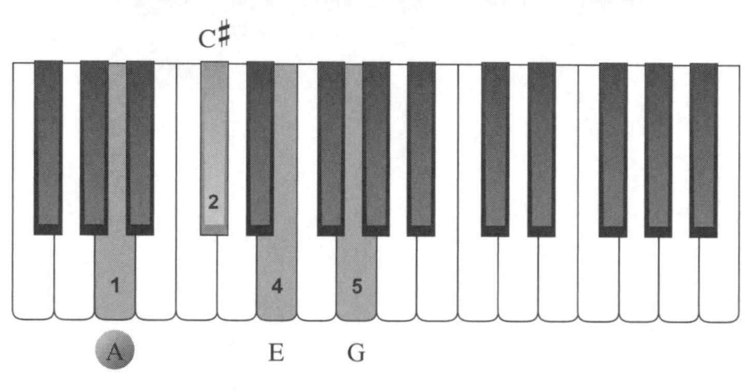

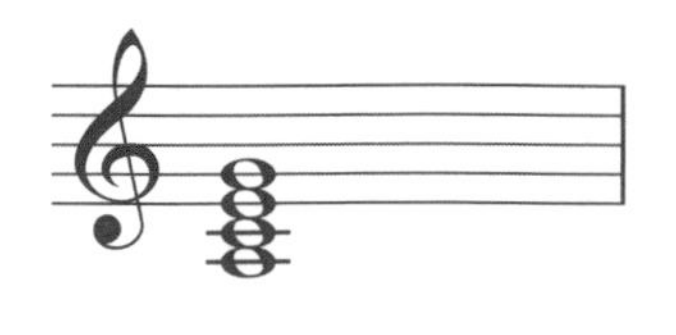

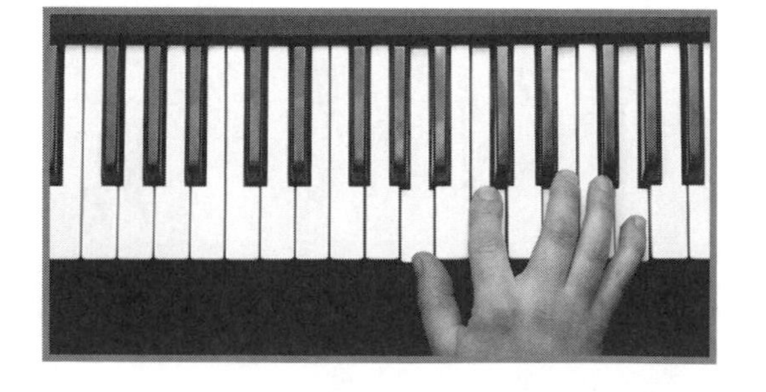

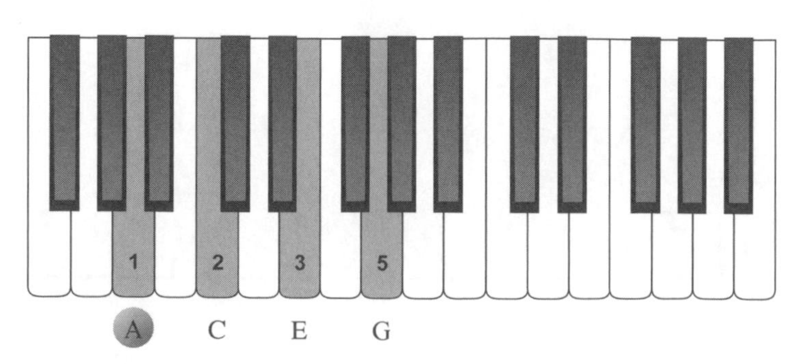

Bmaj^7

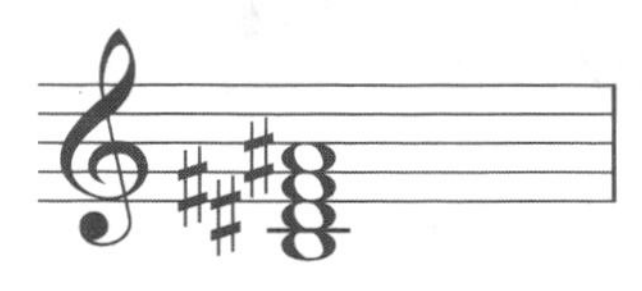

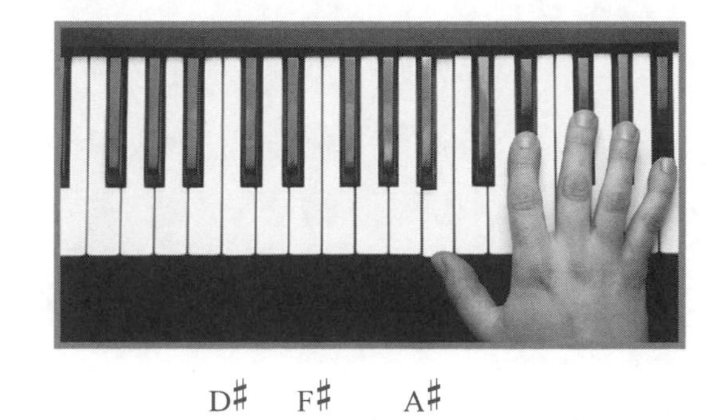

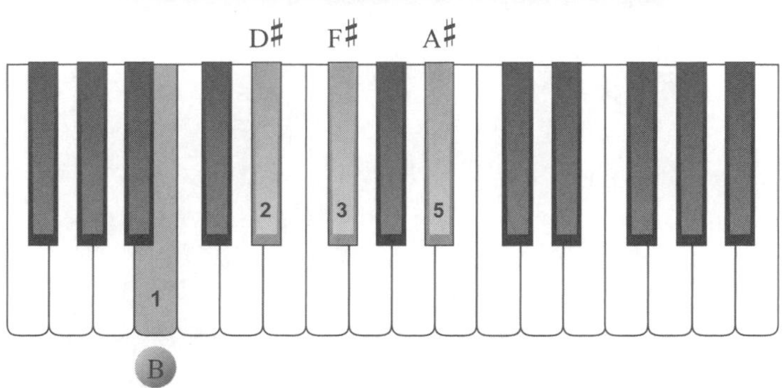

B^7

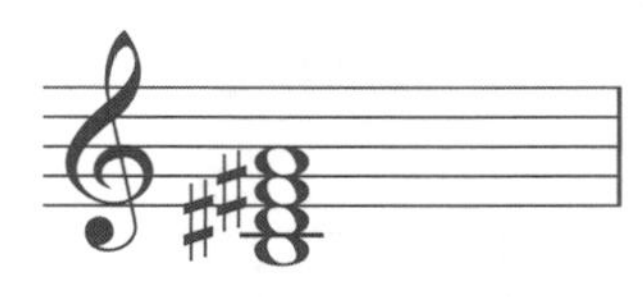

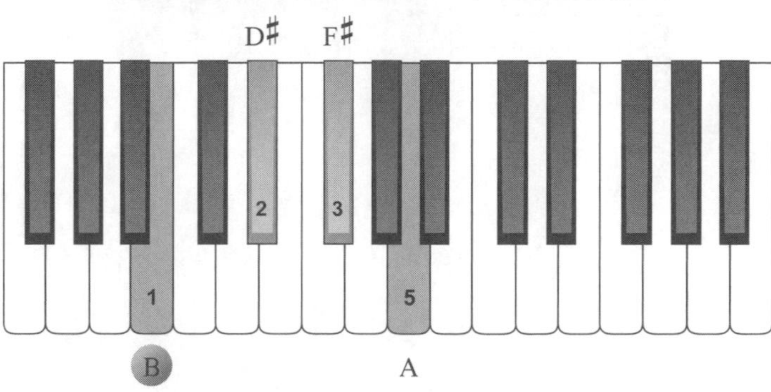

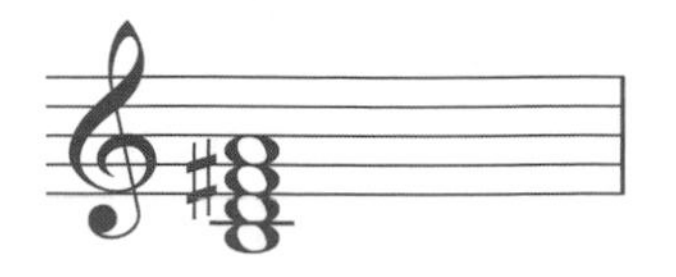

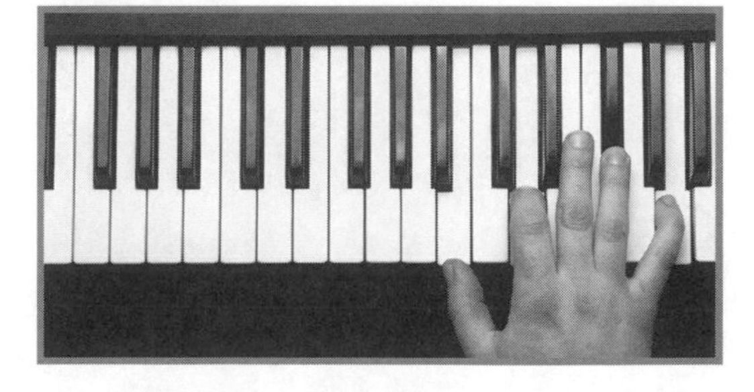

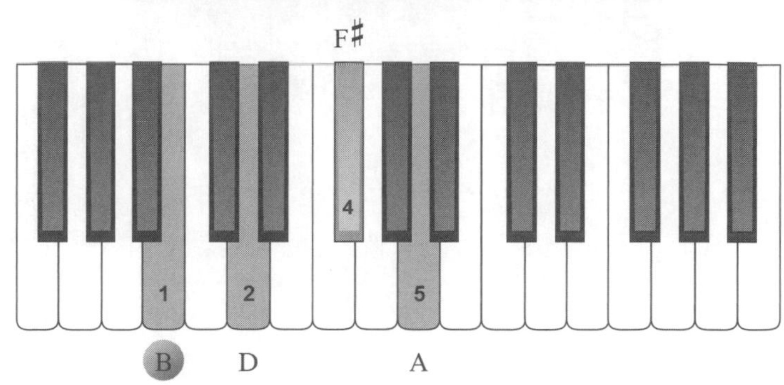

Cmaj^7

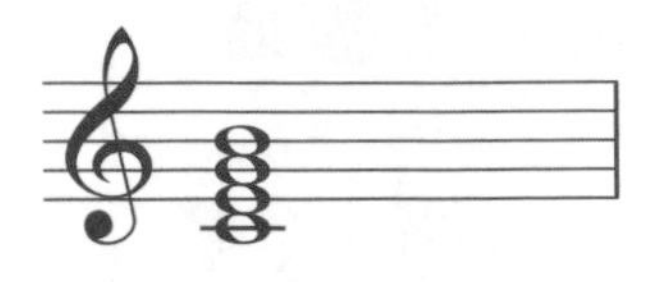

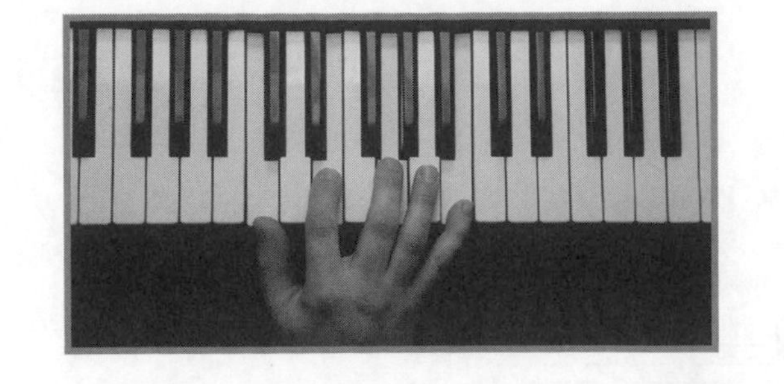

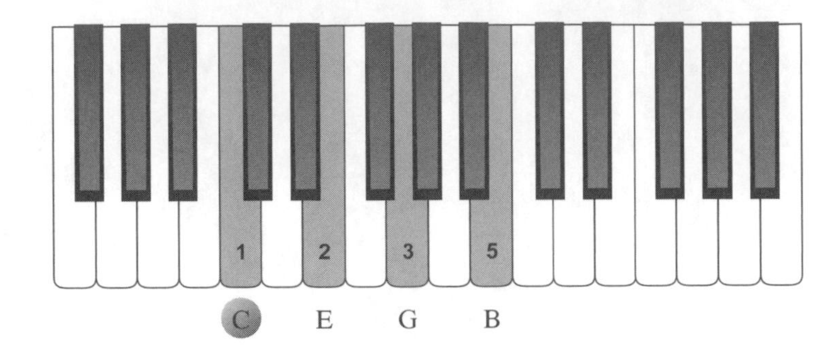

C^7

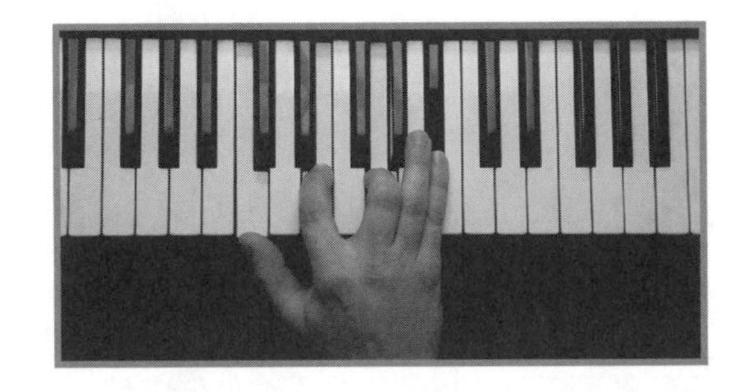

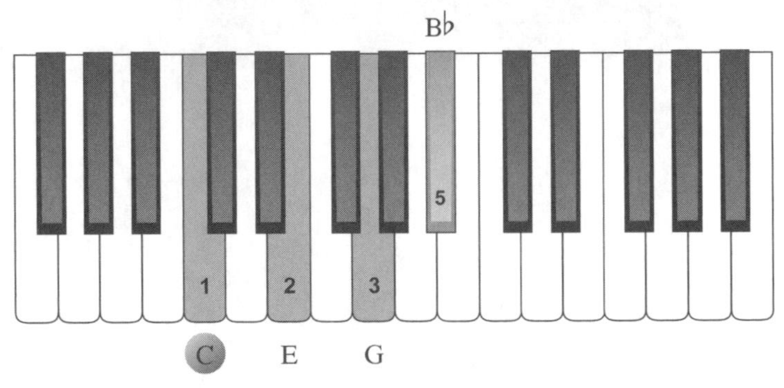

Cm^7

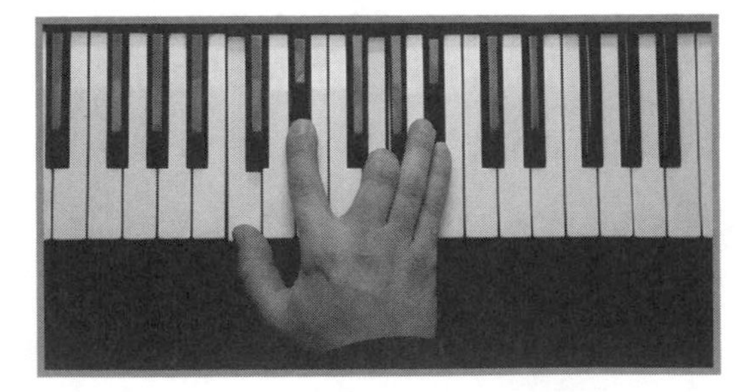

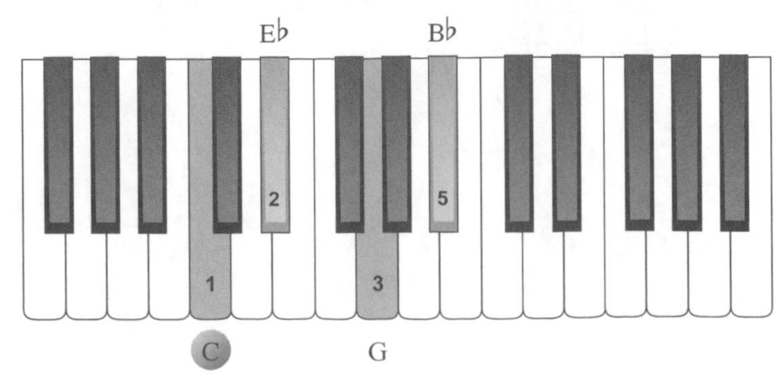

Dmaj^7

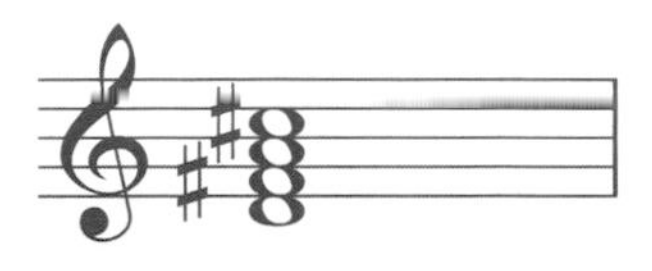

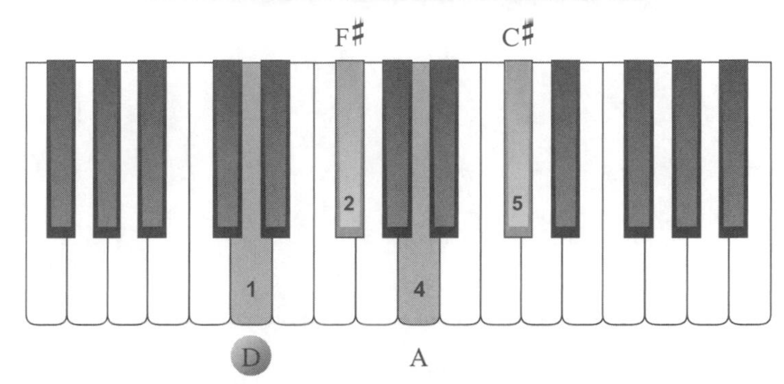

D^7

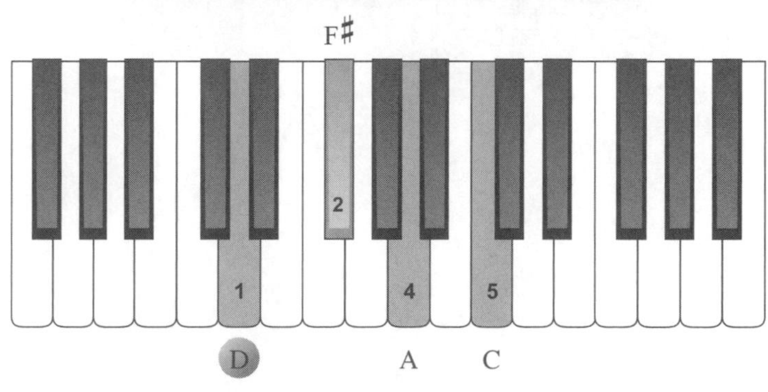

Dm^7

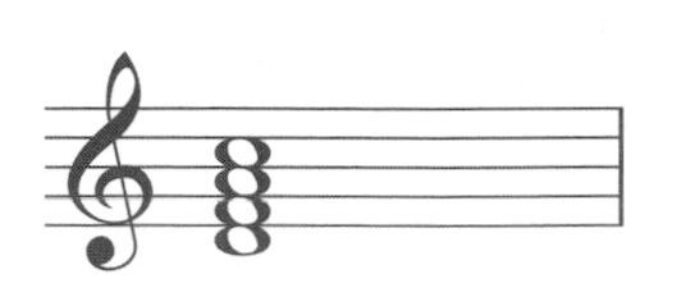

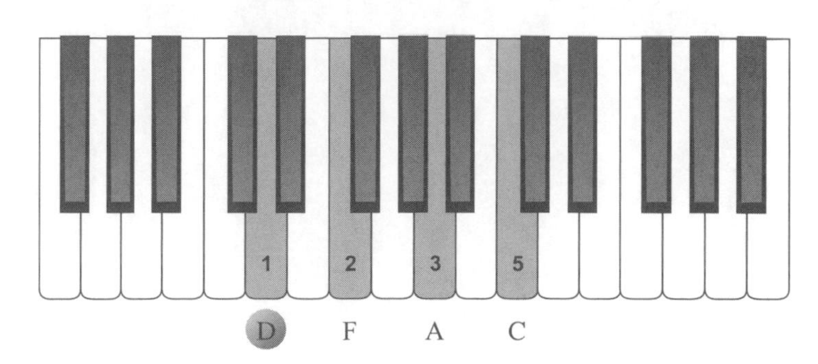

Emaj^7

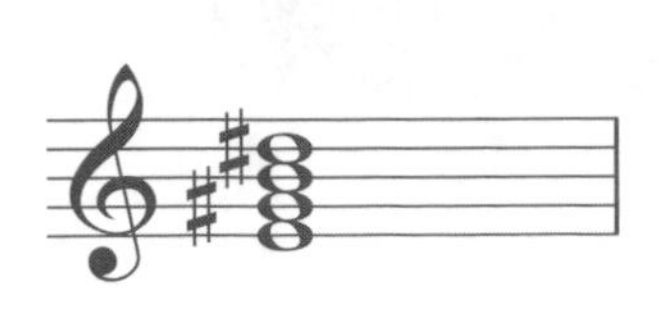

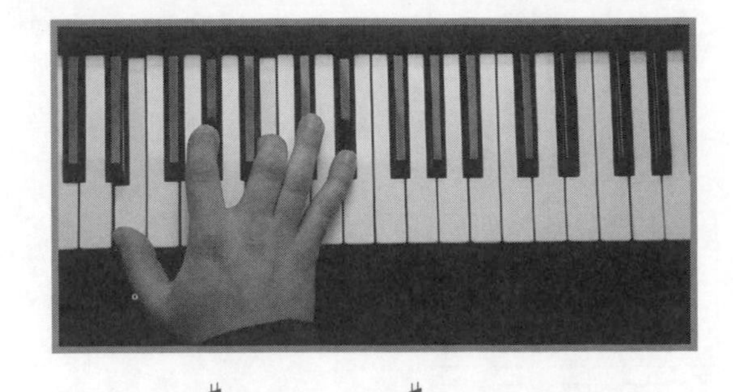

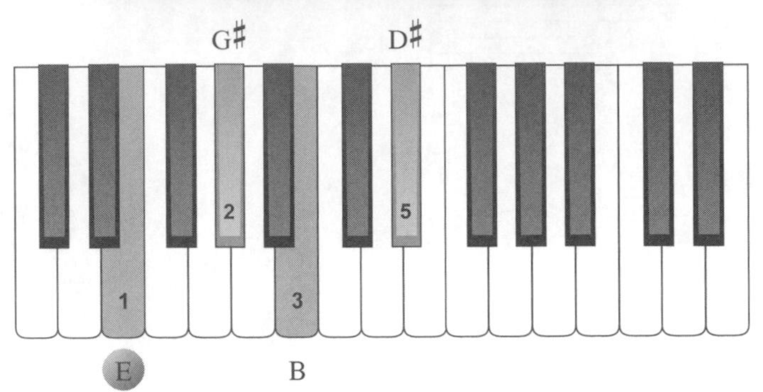

E^7

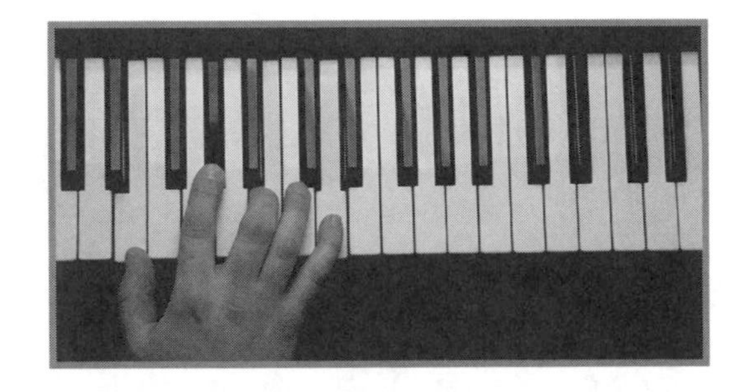

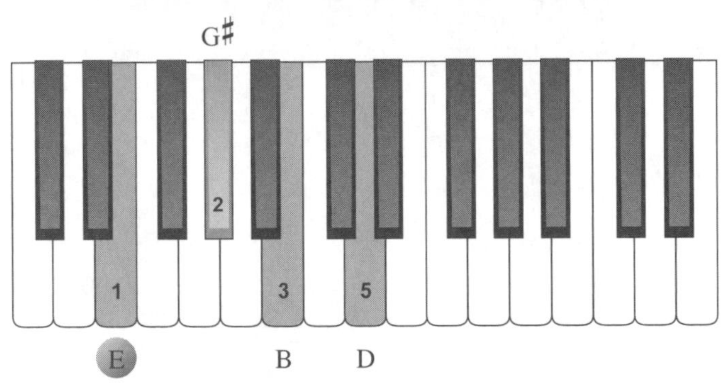

Em^7

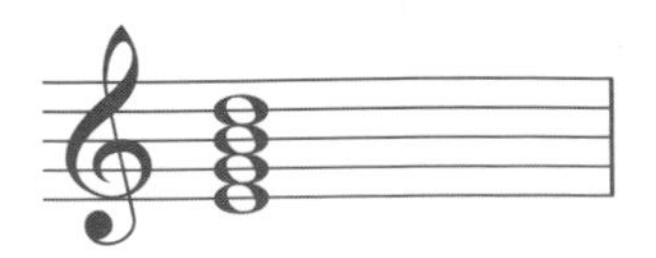

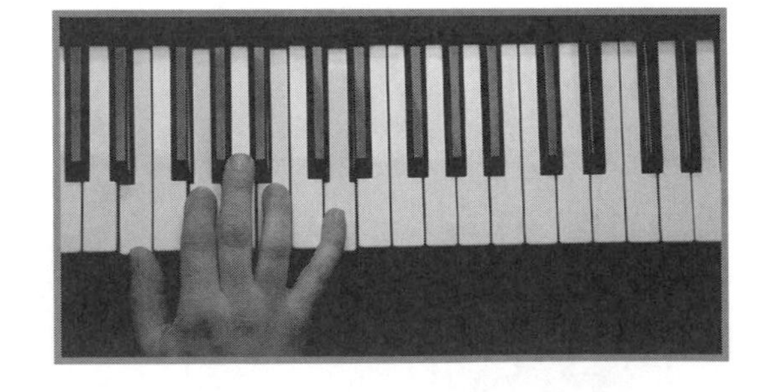

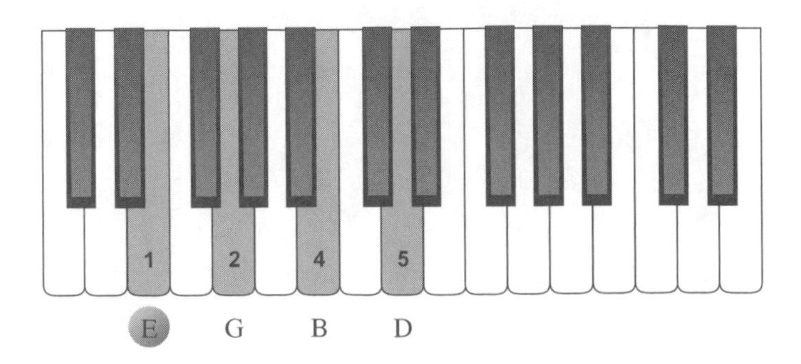

Fmaj^{7}

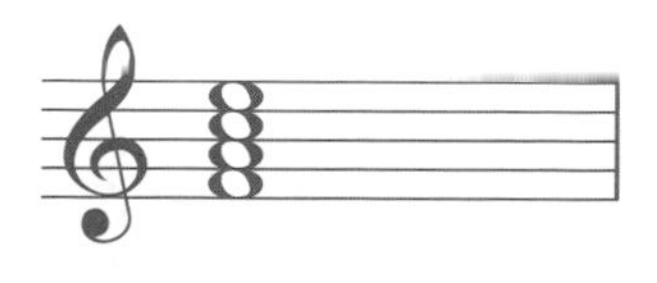

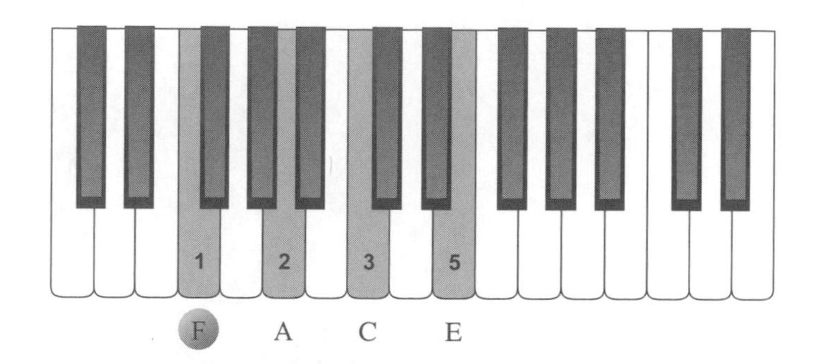

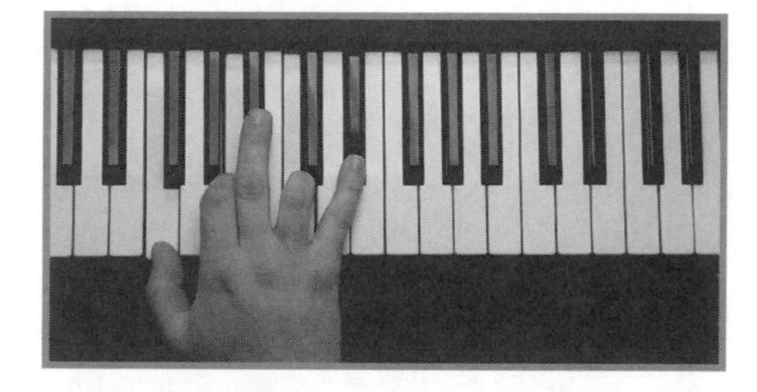

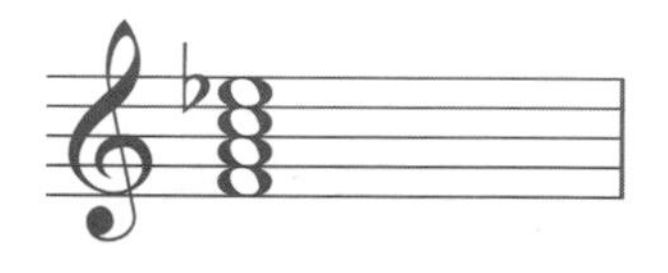

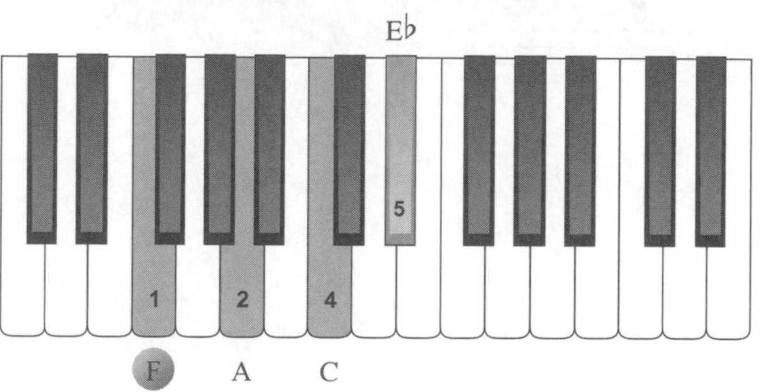

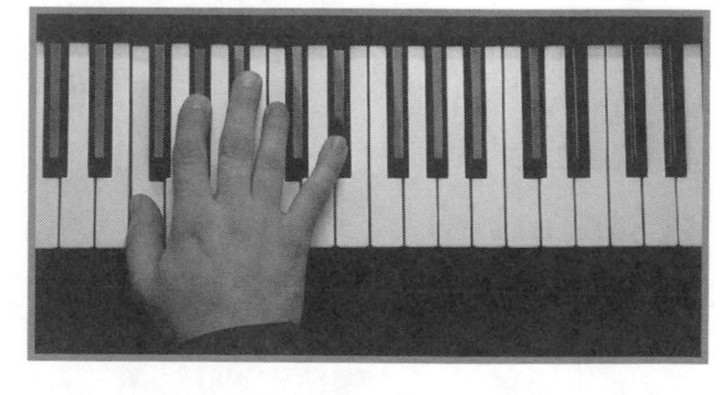

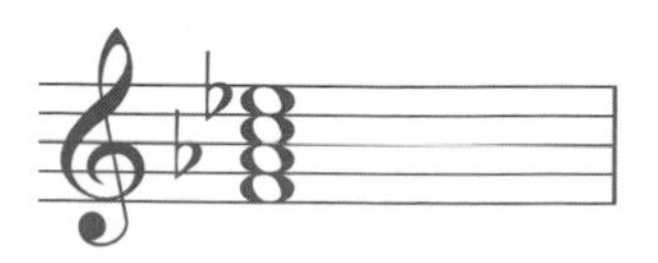

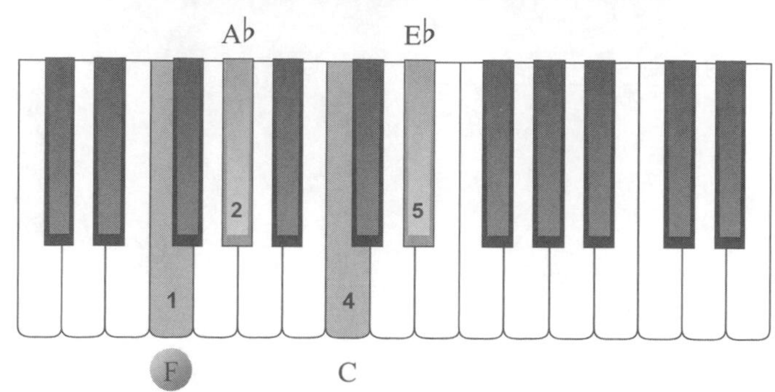

Gmaj^7

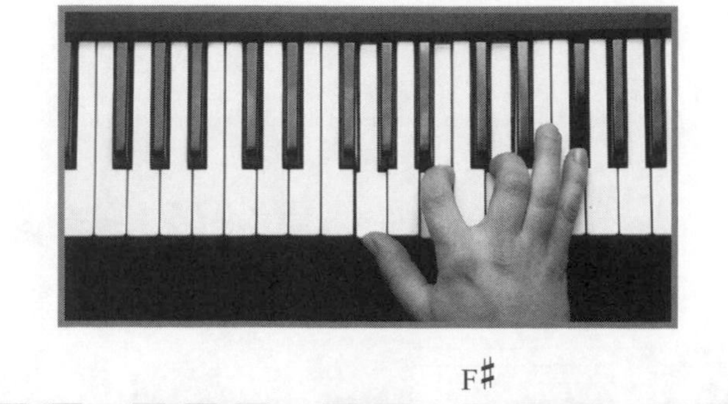

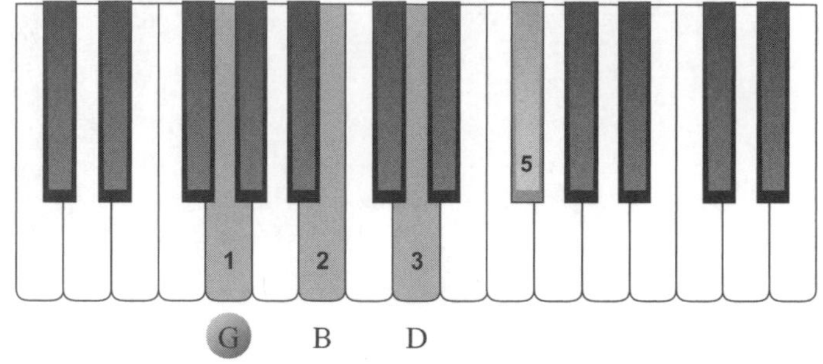

G^7

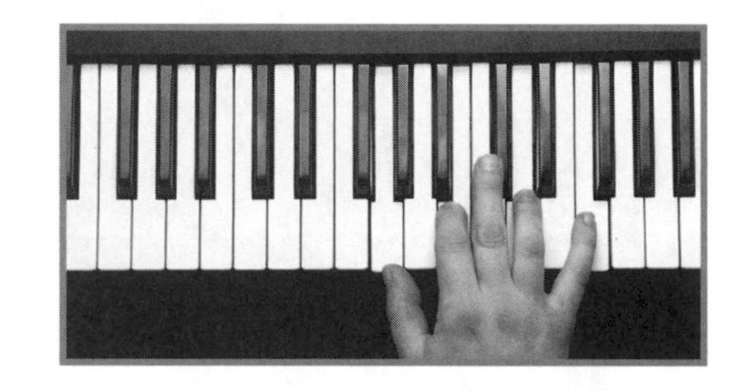

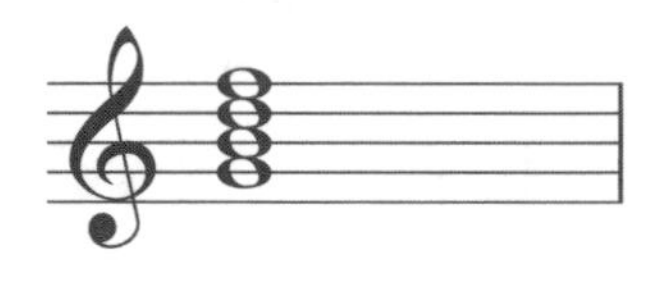

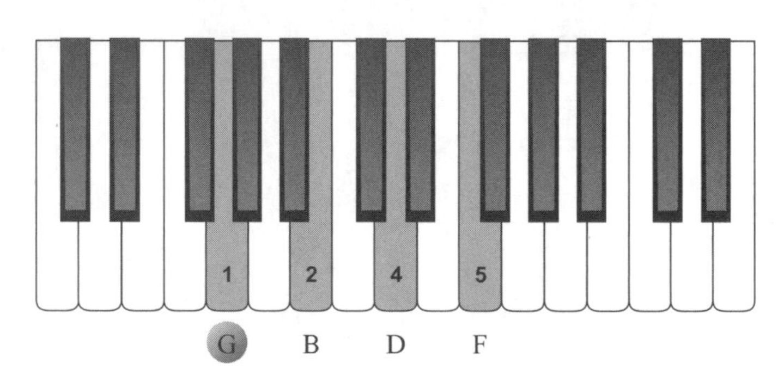

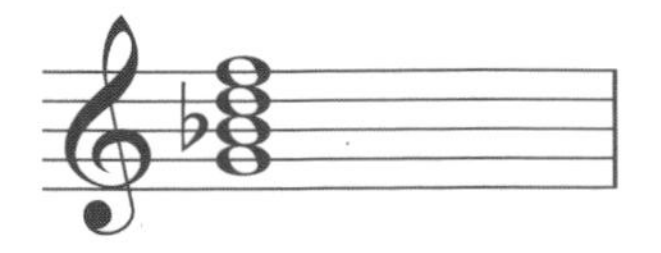

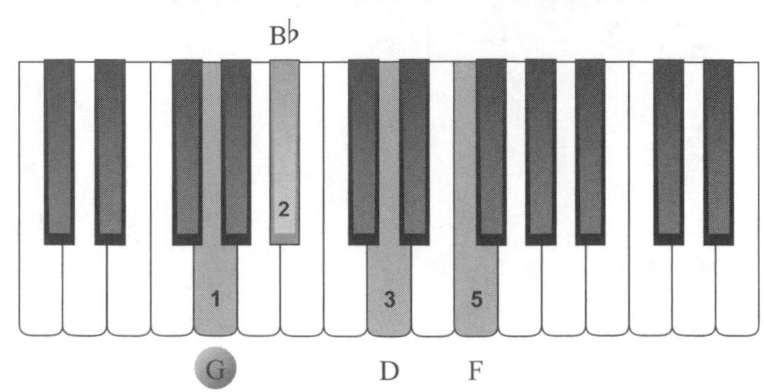

About the Author

John McCarthy
Creator of
The Rock House Method

John is the creator of The Rock House Method®, the world's leading musical instruction system. Over his 25 plus year career, he has written, produced and/or appeared in more than 100 instructional products. Millions of people around the world have learned to play music using John's easy-to-follow, accelerated programs.

John is a virtuoso musician who has worked with some of the industry's most legendary musicians. He has the ability to break down, teach and communicate music in a manner that motivates and inspires others to achieve their dreams of playing an instrument.

As a musician and songwriter, John blends together a unique style of rock, metal, funk and blues in a collage of melodic compositions. Throughout his career, John has recorded and performed with renowned musicians including Doug Wimbish (Joe Satriani, Living Colour, The Rolling Stones, Madonna, Annie Lennox), Grammy Winner Leo Nocentelli, Rock & Roll Hall of Fame inductees Bernie Worrell and Jerome "Big Foot" Brailey, Freekbass, Gary Hoey, Bobby Kimball, David Ellefson (founding member of seven time Grammy nominee Megadeth), Will Calhoun (B.B. King, Mick Jagger and Paul Simon), Gus G of Ozzy and many more.

To get more information about John McCarthy, his music and instructional products visit RockHouseSchool.com.